TOEIC® Strategy

Winning Multiple Choice Strategies for the TOEIC® Exam

Published by

Complete **TEST** Preparation Inc.

ISBN-13: 978-1772450590 (Complete Test Preparation Inc.)
ISBN-10: 1772450596

Version 4.0 January 2018

Published by
Complete Test Preparation Inc.
Victoria BC Canada

Visit us on the web at http://www.test-preparation.ca
Printed in the USA

About Complete Test Preparation Inc.

The Complete Test Preparation Team has been publishing high quality study materials since 2005. Thousands of students visit our websites every year, and thousands of students, teachers and parents all over the world have purchased our teaching materials, curriculum, study guides and practice tests.

Complete Test Preparation is committed to providing students with the best study materials and practice tests available on the market. Members of our team combine years of teaching experience, with experienced writers and editors, all with advanced degrees.

Feedback

We welcome your feedback. Email us at feedback@test-preparation.ca with your comments and suggestions. We carefully review all suggestions and often incorporate reader suggestions into upcoming versions. As a Print on Demand Publisher, we update our products frequently.

 Find us on Facebook

www.facebook.com/CompleteTestPreparation

Contents

Getting Started with the TOEIC®

CONGRATULATIONS! By deciding to take the TOEIC®, you have taken the first step toward a great future! Of course, there is no point in taking this important examination unless you intend to do your best to earn the highest grade that you possibly can. That means getting yourself organized and discovering the best approaches, methods and strategies to master the material. Yes, that will require real effort and dedication on your part, but if you are willing to focus your energy and devote the study time necessary, before you know it you will be finished the exam with a great mark!

We know that taking on a new endeavour can be a little scary, and it is easy to feel unsure of where to begin. That's where we come in. This study guide is designed to help you improve your test-taking skills, show you a few tricks and increase both your competency and confidence.

The TOEIC® Exam

The TOEIC® exam is composed of three sections, reading, listening and writing. The reading section consists of reading comprehension questions. A short passage is given, followed by a series of questions. The listening section consists of listening comprehension questions, where you listen to a short passage and the answer questions. The writing section contains an essay question.

While we seek to make our guide as comprehensive as possible, it is important to note that like all exams, the TOEIC® Exam might be adjusted at some future point. New material might be added, or content that is no longer relevant or applicable might be removed. It is always a good idea to give the materials you receive when you register to take the TOEIC® a careful review.

While we seek to make our guide as comprehensive as possible, note that like all entrance exams, the TOEIC® Exam might be adjusted at some future point. New material might be added, or content that is no longer relevant or applicable might be removed. It is always a good idea to give the materials you receive when you register to take the TOEIC® a careful review.

Test Strategy

This is a book about improving your score by using proven test strategies. This is a little different from other books such as a study guide, or a practice test. Even though we do provide lots of information to study and practice test questions, this book is about how to tackle multiple choice questions.

But do not worry - that is not all! While you are learning different strategies for answering multiple choice questions, you can also practice your reading and listening comprehension skills, plus reveiew tips on how to write an essay, which are more than half your score on the TOEIC®.

A Better Score Is Possible

Worried about that big exam coming up? Do you think you're just not a good test-taker, especially when it comes to standardized tests? The good news is that you're not alone. The bad news is that millions of people are left behind through objective testing, simply because they're not good test-takers - even though they may know the material. They don't know how to handle the format well or understand what's expected of them.

This is especially true of the multiple-choice test. Test-takers are given lots of support for taking essay-style tests. They're helped with skills such as grammar and spelling. However, little is offered for the multiple-choice exam. This is despite the fact that thousands of people find multiple-choice to be the most challenging kind of test. Here are some reasons that so many people have difficulties with multiple-choice:

The Broad Range. Because the questions are so short and quick, a lot of ground is covered in the test. Who's to know what to study with so much material covered?

Time Limits. Most standardized tests have time limits, which adds an extra layer of pressure.

Trickery. Many test-designers think that it is too easy to guess a multiple-choice question correctly, so they intentionally make the questions tricky.

Bluffing Not Allowed. With an essay test, you can try to bluff your way through it. Not so with multiple-choice. The answer is either right or wrong.

Difficult to Write. It's not easy for a test-writer to design a good multiple-choice test. Because of this, sometimes, they make them overly difficult.

Shuffled Content. Multiple-choice tests tend to throw the questions in at random, in no particular order. You could be answering a question about the 1700s and then about the 2004 Presidential election.

These challenges mean that students have to be familiar with a wider range of material than on other kinds of exams. You'll need to know specific vocabulary, rules, names, dates, etc.

There are, however, a few advantages to you, the test-taker, with a multiple-choice test. For instance, because there are more multiple-choice items on a test than there are other types, each question tends to have a lower point value. You can afford to miss a few and still be okay. Also, if you're doing a fill-in-the-blank or essay test, you have to rely totally on memory for the answer. With a multiple-choice exam, you know that the correct answer is somewhere in the question. You just have to decide which one it is. Often, seeing the right answer will trigger your memory, and you'll recognize it instantly.

Keep in mind, though, the test-writer knows that one of the advantages of multiple-choice is the fact the answer is on the page. This leads to many test-writers to include what is called a "distracter." This is a possible answer that is designed to look like the correct answer, but which is actually wrong. We'll talk about this again later, but an example would be the question: "Who is known for posting 95 theses on a church wall?" Among the answers might be Martin Luther and Martin Luther King. Because the student vaguely remembers the name "Martin Luther" from the course materials, there's a chance that he'll select the incorrect "Martin Luther King."

Who Does Well On Multiple-Choice Exams?

With so many challenges working against you on the multiple-choice exam, what's the answer? Is there a way to improve your chances and your score? There is! The point of this book is not to discourage you, but to make you aware that there are strategies and tips that you can incorporate to raise your test score. Before we get into the specific strategies, let's take a general look at who does best on these types of tests.

> **Those who know the material.** This should go without saying, but the thing that will most raise your test score will be if you know the material that's going to be covered. While the strategies we'll discuss later will help you even with questions you're unsure of, the surest thing you can do is learn the rules, dates, names, and concepts that you'll be tested on.

> **Those who have a calm, cool demeanor when taking a test.** Panicking can cause you to forget the information you think you know. Confidence goes a long way toward a better mark on multiple-choice.

> **Those who meditate or pray before the test.** Don't laugh. It's a known fact that people who meditate or pray, depending on their beliefs, enter a test room more confidently, and do better on the exam.

> **Those who operate on logic rather than instinct.** Those who take a multiple-choice test based on instinct

will be tempted to overlook the stated facts, and let emotion rule.

Those who have a system. Most of the book will deal with this, but you should not just guess randomly on questions you don't know. You must have a systematic strategy.

Types of Multiple-Choice Questions

EVEN IF YOU KNOW THAT A TEST WILL BE MULTIPLE-CHOICE, YOU STILL DON'T KNOW ALL THAT YOU NEED TO KNOW. There are various types of multiple-choice questions. Some tests will use just one of these kinds. Others will use several, or even all of them. Let's examine the various types of multiple-choice questions you are likely to encounter.

1. The "Who, What, Where Question." This is the simplest, most basic form of multiple-choice question. It asks for you to recall a single, simple fact about the material. For instance:

Where did the Wright Brothers fly their first airplane?

> a. Richmond, VA
>
> b. Kitty Hawk, NC
>
> c. Charlotte, NC
>
> d. Philadelphia, PA

The correct answer is B. This question simply asks for you to correctly identify a place name.

2. The "Multiple-Answer" Multiple-choice Question. This one varies from the "Who, What, Where" question in that more than one answer could be correct. It often appears like this:

Which of the following was not a declared war by the U.S. Congress?

I.   World War I

II. World War II

III. The Korean War

IV. The Vietnam War

    a. I only

    b. I and II only

    c. III only

    d. IV only

    e. III and IV only

The correct answer here is E; neither the Korean nor Vietnam Wars were declared a war by Congress. These questions are tricky because many people are tempted, when they see a right answer, to select it, without thinking that there might be another answer that's also right.

3. The "Best Answer" Multiple-choice Question. On this type, the there might not be one clear objective answer, but rather, you're required to select the one that comes closest to being right, or closest to what you believe is right. For example:

The factor which was the most to blame for the 1986 explosion of the Space Shuttle Challenger was:

    a. It launched too early in the morning.

    b. The cold weather allowed ice to develop.

    c. The astronauts did not have enough sleep.

    d. The astronauts were not adequately trained.

While it's entirely possible that C or D might have played a role, it's now commonly believed that the cause was the ice which had built up on the Shuttle's "O" rings. Some answers are possible, but B is the best answer.

4. The "Fill in the Blank" Multiple-choice Question. This is frequently used on both grammar and reading comprehension tests. The question is presented as a sentence, with one or two key words left out. You must choose the correct one to fill the blank. Example:

The animals at the zoo _____ by the visitors.

   a. Did not feed
   b. Cannot fed
   c. Should not be fed
   d. Never feeding

The answer is C, since "The animals at the zoo should not be fed by the visitors" is the only one which makes good, grammatical sense.

Most the multiple-choice questions you'll encounter will fall into one above category, although it's possible you might also encounter a strange hybrid of two or three types. During your practice for the test, you should practice on each of these four types.

Multiple-Choice Quick Tips

Before looking at specific strategies in detail, lets first look at some general tips that you can use on any test and on multiple-choice questions in any subject. We will explore some of these in more detail later.

• **Finding Hints without Cheating** Pssst. There is a way to get hints about a question, even as you are taking the test—and it is completely legal. The key: Use the test itself to find clues about the answer. Here is how to do this. If you find that a question stumps you, read the answers. If you find one that uses the language that your teacher or textbook used, there is a good chance that this is the right answer. That is because on complex topics, teachers and books tend to always use the same or similar language.

Another point: Look out for test questions which are like previous questions. Often, you will find the same information used in more than one question.

Occasionally you will find the answer to one question contained in another question - be on the lookout for this type of situation and use it to your advantage.

• **Before you try eliminating wrong answers, try to solve the problem.** If you know for sure that you have answered the question correctly, then obviously there is no need to eliminate wrong choices. If you cannot solve it, then see how many choices you can eliminate. Now try solving it again and see if one of the remaining answers comes close to your answer. Your chances of getting the answer right have now improved dramatically. Elimination is one of the most powerful strategies and we will discuss in more detail, as well as practice below.

• **Skip if you do not know.** If you simply do not know the answer and do not know how to get the answer, mark the question in the margin and come back if you have time.

• **Rule out answers that seem so general that they do not offer much information.** If an answer said, for example, "Columbus came to the West in the spring," it is probably not the right answer.

• **Use "all of the above" and "none of the above" to your advantage.** For "all of the above," you need not check to make sure all options are correct. Just check two of them. If two of the answers are correct, then this probably means they are all correct, and you can select "all." (This, of course, is not always the case, especially if there is also an option for "A and B" or "C and D."). Similarly, with "all of the above" questions, you only have to find one wrong answer, and then you have eliminated two choices - one is the wrong answer, and the other is All of the Above.

• **Let "close" answers be your guide.** The clever test-writer often includes an answer that is almost the correct one, to throw you off. The clever test-taker, however, can use this to his advantage. If you see two options that are strangely similar, then chances are good that one of those is the correct choice. That means you can rule out the other answers—and thus improve your chances. For instance, if two choices are George Washington and George Washington Carver, among Abraham Lincoln and Thomas Edison, there is a good chance that one of the two Washingtons is right. More on this strategy below.

Watch Out For Trick Questions

In general, most questions are what they appear to be and over-analyzing is a pitfall to be avoided. However, most multiple-choice tests contain one or two trick questions for a variety of reasons. A trick question is one where the test-writer intentionally makes you think that the answer is easier than it really is. Test-writers include trick questions because so many people think that they have mastered the techniques of taking a test that they need not study the material. In only a very few cases will a test have more than a handful of trick questions. Often instructors will include trick questions, where you really have to know your stuff inside-out to answer it correctly. This separates the "A" students from the "B+" students, and the "A" students from the "A+" students.

The best way to beat the trick question is to read the question carefully and break it down into parts. Then break it down into individual words. For instance, if a question asks,

> "When a plane crashes on the border between the United States and Canada, where are the survivors buried?"

if you had looked at each word individually, you would have realized that the last word, "survivors," means that the test writer is talking about burying people who are still alive.

Before You Change That Answer ...

You are probably familiar with the concept by now: your first instinct is usually right. That is why so many people, when giving advice about tests, tell you that unless you are convinced that your first instinct was wrong, do not take a chance. In those cases, more people change a right answer to the wrong one more often than they change a wrong answer to a right one.

How to Handle This.

Let's take that advice a step further, though. Maybe you do not always have to leave your first answer, especially if you think there might be a reasonable chance that your second choice was right. Before you go changing the answer, though, go on and do a few questions and clear your thoughts of the problem question. After you have done a few more, go back and start over from the beginning. Then see if the original answer is still the one that jumps out at you. If so, leave it. If your second thought now jumps out at you, then go ahead and change it. If both are equal in your mind, then leave it with your first hunch.

Answering Multiple-Choice Step-by-Step

HERE IS A TEST QUESTION:

Which of the following is a helpful tip for taking a multiple-choice test?

    a. Answering "B" for all questions.

    b. Eliminate all answers that you know cannot be true.

    c. Eliminate all answers that seem like they might be true.

    d. Cheat off your neighbor.

If you answered B, you are correct. Even if you are not positive about the answer, try to get rid of as many options as possible. Think of it this way: If every item on your test has four possible answers, and if you guess on one of those four answers, you have a one-in-four chance (25%) of getting it right. This means you should get one question right for every four that you guess.

However, if you can get rid of two answers, then your chances improve to one-in-two chances, or 50%. That means you will get a correct answer for every two that you guess.

So much for an obvious tip for improving your multiple-choice score. There are many other tips that you may or may not have considered, which will give your grade a boost. Remember, though, that none of these tips are infallible. In fact, some test-writers who know these suggestions deliberately write questions that can confound your system. Usually, however, you will do better on the test if you put these tips into practice.

By familiarizing yourself with these tips, you increase your chances and who knows; you might just get a lucky break and increase your score by a few points!

Answering Step-by-Step.

It might seem complicated and unnecessary to follow a formula for answering a multiple-choice question. After you have practiced this formula for a while, though, it will come naturally and will not take any time at all. Try to follow these steps below on each question.

Step 1. Cover up the answers while you read the question. See the material in your mind's eye and try to envision what the correct answer is before you expose the answers on the answer sheet.

Step 2. Uncover the responses.

Step 3. Eliminate or Estimate. Cross out every choice that you know is ridiculous, absurd or clearly wrong. Then work with the answers that remain.

Step 4. Watch for distracters. A distracter is an answer that looks very similar to the correct answer, but is put there to trip you up. If you see two answers that are strikingly similar, the chances are good that one of them is correct. For instance, if you are asked the term for the distance around a square, and two of the responses are "periwinkle" and "perimeter," you can guess that one of these is probably correct, since the words look similar (both start with "peri-"). Guess one of these two and your chances of correcting selecting "perimeter" are 50/50. More on this below.

Step 5. Check! If you see the answer that you saw in your mind, put a light check-mark by it and then see if any of the other choices are better. If not, mark that response as your answer.

Step 6. If all else fails, guess. If you cannot envision the correct response in your head, or figure it out by reading the passage, and if you are left totally clueless as to what the answer should be, guess.

The TOEIC does not penalize for wrong answers, so if all else fails, guessing is a good strategy.

There is a common myth that says choice "C" has a statistically greater chance of being correct. This may be true if your professor is making the test, however, most standardized tests today are generated by computer and the choices are randomized. We do not recommend choosing "C" as a strategy.

That is a quick introduction to multiple-choice to get us warmed up. Next we move onto the strategies and practice test questions section. Each multiple-choice strategy is explained, followed by practice questions using the strategy. Opposite this page is a bubble sheet for answering.

MULTIPLE-CHOICE STRATEGY PRACTICE QUESTIONS ANSWER SHEET.

	A B C D E		A B C D E
1	○ ○ ○ ○ ○	26	○ ○ ○ ○ ○
2	○ ○ ○ ○ ○	27	○ ○ ○ ○ ○
3	○ ○ ○ ○ ○	28	○ ○ ○ ○ ○
4	○ ○ ○ ○ ○	29	○ ○ ○ ○ ○
5	○ ○ ○ ○ ○	30	○ ○ ○ ○ ○
6	○ ○ ○ ○ ○	31	○ ○ ○ ○ ○
7	○ ○ ○ ○ ○	32	○ ○ ○ ○ ○
8	○ ○ ○ ○ ○	33	○ ○ ○ ○ ○
9	○ ○ ○ ○ ○	34	○ ○ ○ ○ ○
10	○ ○ ○ ○ ○	35	○ ○ ○ ○ ○
11	○ ○ ○ ○ ○	36	○ ○ ○ ○ ○
12	○ ○ ○ ○ ○	37	○ ○ ○ ○ ○
13	○ ○ ○ ○ ○	38	○ ○ ○ ○ ○
14	○ ○ ○ ○ ○	39	○ ○ ○ ○ ○
15	○ ○ ○ ○ ○	40	○ ○ ○ ○ ○
16	○ ○ ○ ○ ○	41	○ ○ ○ ○ ○
17	○ ○ ○ ○ ○	42	○ ○ ○ ○ ○
18	○ ○ ○ ○ ○	43	○ ○ ○ ○ ○
19	○ ○ ○ ○ ○	44	○ ○ ○ ○ ○
20	○ ○ ○ ○ ○	45	○ ○ ○ ○ ○
21	○ ○ ○ ○ ○		
22	○ ○ ○ ○ ○		
23	○ ○ ○ ○ ○		
24	○ ○ ○ ○ ○		
25	○ ○ ○ ○ ○		

Multiple-Choice Strategy Practice Questions

THE FOLLOWING ARE DETAILED STRATEGIES FOR ANSWERING MULTIPLE-CHOICE QUESTIONS WITH PRACTICE QUESTIONS FOR EACH STRATEGY.

Answers appear following this section with a detailed explanation and discussion on each strategy and question, plus tips and analysis.

Strategy 1 - Locate Keywords

For every question, figure out exactly what the question is asking by locating key words that are in the question. Underline the keywords to clarify your thoughts and keep on track.

Directions: Read the passage below, and answer the questions using this strategy.

Free-range is a method of farming where animals are allowed to roam freely, instead of being enclosed in a pen. The term is used in two senses that do not overlap completely: as a farmer-centric description of farming methods, and as a consumer-centric description. Farmers practice free-range to achieve free-range or humane certification (and thus capture high prices), to reduce feed costs, to improve the happiness and liveliness of their animals, to produce a higher-quality product, and as a method of raising multiple crops on the same land. [1]

1. The free-range method of farming

a. Uses a minimum amount of fencing to give animals more room.

b. Can refer to two different things.

c. Is always a very humane method.

d. Only allows for one crop at a time.

2. Free-range farming is practiced

a. To obtain free-range certification.

b. To lower the cost of feeding animals.

c. To produce higher quality product.

d. All of the above.

3. Free-range farming:

a. Can mean either farmer described or consumer described methods.

b. Is becoming much more popular in many areas.

c. Has many limits and causes prices to go down.

d. Is only done to make the animals happier and healthier.

4. Free-range certification is most important to farmers because:

a. Free-range livestock are less expensive to feed.

b. The price of the product is higher.

c. Both a and b

d. The animals are kept in smaller enclosures, so more can be produced.

Strategy 2 - Watch Negatives

For every question, no matter what type, look for negatives. These can include never, not, and others that will completely change what is being asked.

Directions: Read the passage below, and answer the questions using this strategy.

Male grizzly bears can weight more than 1,000 pounds, but typically weigh 400 pounds to 770 pounds. Females are on average 38% smaller, about 250–350 pounds, an example of sexual dimorphism. On average, grizzly bears stand about 1 meter (3.3 ft.) at the shoulder when on all fours, and 2 meters (6.6 ft.) on their hind legs, but males often stand 2.44 meters (8 ft.) or more on their hind legs. On average, grizzly bears from the Yukon River area are about 20% smaller than typical grizzlies. [2]

5. Sexual dimorphism does not mean

    a. Male grizzly bears are the same size as the female of the species.

    b. All grizzly bears look the same and are the same size.

    c. Grizzly bears can be quite large, and weigh more than half a ton.

    d. All of the above

6. The size of a full-grown grizzly bear is never

    a. More than 500 pounds.

    b. Depends on the bear's sex.

    c. Determined simply by diet.

    d. Less than 8 feet tall.

7. Grizzly bears from the area of the Yukon River do not

    a. Get as big as most other grizzly bears do

    b. Get the rich and varied food supply needed

    c. Need the same nutrients as other grizzly bears

    d. Get less than 7 feet tall, and weigh close to half of a ton

Strategy 3 - Read the Stem Completely

For every question, no matter what type, read the information in the stem and then try to determine the correct answer before you look at the different answers.

Directions: Read the passage below, and answer the questions using this strategy.

Formerly, taxonomists listed brown and grizzly bears as separate species. Technically, brown and grizzly bears are classified as the same species, Ursus Arctos. The term "brown bear" is commonly used to refer to the members of this species found in coastal areas where salmon is the primary food source. Brown bears found inland and in northern habitats are often called "grizzlies." Brown bears on Kodiak Island are classified as a distinct subspecies from those on the mainland because they are genetically and physically isolated. The shape of their skulls also differs slightly. [3]

8. Grizzly bears, brown bears, and kodiak bears are all

    a. Arctas Ursinas

    b. Ursus Arctos

    c. Arctos Ursina

    d. Ursula Arctic

9. Kodiak brown bears are classified as a different subspecies because

a. They are much larger than other brown bears

b. Their diet is radically different from that of other brown bears

c. They are not true brown bears but instead a mixture of bear species

d. Of their genetics and head shape, as well as their physical isolation

10. The term grizzlies, when referring to the brown bear, is used mainly

a. In eastern areas where the bear grows large

b. Only in snowy areas where there are low year round temperatures

c. In the northern and inland areas

d. In areas where the bear has a silver appearance

11. The term brown bear is normally used

a. When one of the main food sources is salmon

b. When the bear is small

c. When the bear is found inland

d. When the bear has a light brown coat and is very large

Strategy 4 - Consider all the Choices Before Deciding

For every question, no matter what type, make sure to read every option before making your choice.

Directions: Read the passage below, and answer the questions using this strategy.

Jim Martell, a hunter from Idaho, reportedly found and shot a grizzly-polar bear hybrid near Sachs Harbor on Banks Island, Northwest Territories, Canada, on April 16, 2006. Martell had been hunting for polar bears with an official license and a guide, at a cost of $50,000, and killed the animal believing it to be a normal polar bear. Officials took interest in the creature after noticing that it had thick, creamy white fur, typical of polar bears, as well as long claws; a humped back; a shallow face; and brown patches around its eyes, nose, and back, as well as patches on one foot, which are all traits of grizzly bears. If the bear had been adjudicated to be a grizzly, he would have faced a possible CAN$1,000 fine and up to a year in jail. A DNA test conducted by the Wildlife Genetics International in British Columbia confirmed that it was a hybrid, with the mother a polar bear and the father a grizzly. It is the first documented case in the wild, though it was known that this hybrid was biologically possible and other hybrids have been bred in zoos in the past. [4]

12. Which grizzly bear features did the hybrid bear have?

a. Brown patches in certain areas

b. Long claws

c. A shallow face

d. All of the above

13. The hybrid bear was the result of

a. A male brown bear and a female grizzly.

b. A female brown bear and a male grizzly bear.

c. A female polar bear and a male grizzly bear.

d. A male polar bear and a female grizzly.

14. The hybrid bear tested here was

a. The first case ever known where two different bear species mated successfully.

b. Genetically flawed and prone to many diseases and conditions.

c. A fluke, and a mistake of nature which has never happened.

d. The first proof of a wild bear hybrid species outside zoos.

15. Modern science

> a. Has proven that the cubs from two different species will not survive in almost every case.
>
> b. Has known for some time that these hybrid bears were possible.
>
> c. Completely understands how bear hybrids occur and why this happens in nature.
>
> d. Has studied hundreds of bear hybrids in an attempt to learn more.

Strategy 5 - Elimination

For every question, no matter what type, eliminating obviously incorrect answers narrows the possible choices. Elimination is probably the most powerful strategy for answering multiple-choice.

Directions: Read the passage below, and answer the questions using this strategy.

The male peafowl, or peacock, has long been known and valued for its brilliant tail feathers. The bright spots on it are known as "eyes," and inspired the Greek myth that Hera placed the hundred eyes of the slain giant Argus on the tail of her favorite bird. Indian Peafowl are iridescent blue-green or blue in the head, neck and breast.

The back, or scapular, feathers are vermiculated in black and white, while the primaries are orange-chestnut. The so-called "tail" of the peacock, also termed the "train," is not the tail quill feathers but highly elongated upper tail feathers. It is mostly bronze-green, with a series of eyes that are best seen when the train is fanned. The actual tail feathers are short and grey-colored and can be seen from behind when a peacock's train is fanned in a courtship display.

During the molting season, the males shed their stunning train feathers and reveal the unassuming grey-colored tail, which is normally hidden from view beneath the train. The female peacock is duller in comparison. It is mostly brown, with pale under-parts and some green iridescence in the neck, and lacks the long upper tail feathers of the male. [5]

16. The long colorful tail feathers of the peacock

    a. Are only present in the male of the species

    b. Are used by both sexes to warn off predators

    c. Are normally red and blue in color

    d. Are only present for a very short time each year

17. The differences between the male and female peacock are

    a. Size and weight

    b. Coloring and tail feather length

    c. The female does not ever leave the nest

    d. The male sits on and hatches the eggs

18. The term peacock actually refers to

    a. Both sexes from the pheasant family

    b. The eyes on the tail feathers of the bird

    c. The male bird of the peafowl species

    d. The female bird of the peafowl species

19. The gray tail feathers on the male peacock can be seen

    a. When the bird is startled

    b. Only when the bird is searching for food

    c. When the peacock lowers the tail feathers to the ground

    d. During molting

Strategy 6 - Opposites

For every question, no matter what type, look at answers that are opposites. When two answers are opposites, the odds increase that one of them is the correct answer.

Directions: Read the passage below, and answer the questions using this strategy.

Tennen

Smallpox is an infectious disease unique to humans, caused by either of two virus variants, the Variola Major or Variola Minor. The disease is also known by the Latin names Variola or Variola vera, which is a derivative of the Latin varius, meaning spotted.

Smallpox localizes in small blood vessels of the skin and in the mouth and throat. In the skin, this results in a characteristic rash, and later, blisters. Variola Major produces a more serious disease and has an overall mortality rate of 30–35%. Variola Minor causes a milder form of disease (also known as alastrim, cottonpox, milkpox, whitepox, and Cuban itch) which kills about 1% of its victims. Long-term complications of Variola major infection include characteristic scars, commonly on the face, which occur in 65–85% of survivors. Blindness and limb deformities due to arthritis and osteomyelitis are less common complications, seen in about 2–5% of cases. [6]

20. Smallpox

   a. Effects all mammals, including humans

   b. Is caused by a bacteria from contact with dead flesh

   c. Was called the great pox during the fifteenth century

   d. Only affects humans, although other species can carry and transmit the virus

21. Smallpox caused by Variola major has a

   a. Thirty to thirty five percent survival rate

   b. Sixty percent mortality rate

   c. Thirty to thirty five percent mortality rate

   d. Sixty percent survival rate

22. Smallpox caused by Variola minor is

a. Much more severe, with a greater number of pox and more scarring

b. Much less severe, with fewer pox and less scarring

c. Characterized because there are no pox

d. So minor that no treatment or medical attention is needed

23. Smallpox can be fatal

a. In between thirty and thirty five percent of those who catch the virus, depending on the type

b. In between thirty and sixty five percent of those who catch the virus, depending on the type

c. When no medical treatment is available

d. Only in developing countries where medical care is poor

Strategy 7 - Look for Differences

For every question, no matter what type, look at the two choices that seem to be correct and then examine the differences between the two. Refer to the stem to determine the best answer.

Directions: Read the passage below, and answer the questions using this strategy.

Lightning is an atmospheric discharge of electricity accompanied by thunder, which typically occurs during thunderstorms, and sometimes during volcanic eruptions or dust storms. Atmospheric electrical discharges, or bolts of lightning, can travel at speeds of 130,000 mph, and reach temperatures approaching 54,000° F. This is hot enough to fuse silica sand into glass channels, known as fulgurites, that are normally hollow and can extend some distance into the ground. There are some 16 million lightning storms in the world every year.

The irrational fear of lightning and thunder is astraphobia.

Lightning can also occur within the ash clouds of volcanic

eruptions, or can be caused by violent forest fires which generate sufficient dust to create a static charge.

How lightning initially forms is still a matter of debate: Scientists have studied root causes ranging from atmospheric perturbations (wind, humidity, friction, and atmospheric pressure) to the impact of solar wind and accumulation of charged solar particles. Ice inside a cloud is thought to be a key element in lightning development, and may cause a forcible separation of positive and negative charges within the cloud, thus helping in the formation of lightning. [z]

24. Astraphobia is

    a. Fear of thunder

    b. Fear of thunder and lightning

    c. Fear of lightning

    d. None of the above

25. Lightning occurs

    a. Only in thunderstorms

    b. In thunderstorms and dust storms

    c. In thunderstorms, volcanic eruptions and dust storms

    d. In the upper atmosphere

26. Fulgurites are

    a. Made of silica

    b. Made of glass

    c. Made of silica turned in to glass

    d. Made of silica and glass

Strategy 8 - Context clues

Look at the sentences and the context to determine the best
option. Sometimes, the answer may be located right in the passage or question.

**Directions: Read the passage below, and answer the ques-
tions using this strategy.**

Venus is one of the four solar terrestrial planets, meaning that,
like the Earth, it is a rocky body. In size and mass, it is very
similar to the Earth, and is often described as its "sister," or
Earth's twin. The diameter of Venus is only 650 km. less than
the Earth's, and its mass is 81.5% of the Earth's. However,
conditions on the Venusian surface differ radically from those
on Earth, due to its dense carbon dioxide atmosphere. The
mass of the atmosphere of Venus is 96.5% carbon dioxide,
with most of the remaining 3.5% nitrogen.

Venus is the second-closest planet to the Sun, orbiting every
224.7 Earth days. The planet is named after Venus, the Roman
goddess of love and beauty. After the Moon, it is the brightest
natural object in the night sky, reaching an apparent magnitude of −4.6. Because Venus is an inferior planet from Earth,
it never appears to venture far from the Sun: its elongation
reaches a maximum of 47.8°. Venus reaches its maximum
brightness shortly before sunrise or shortly after sunset, and
is often called the Morning Star or the Evening Star. [8]

27. Apparent magnitude is

    a. A measure of darkness

    b. A measure of brightness

    c. The distance from the moon

    d. The distance from the earth

28. The elongation of a planet is

    a. The angular distance from the sun, as seen from earth.

    b. The distance from the sun

    c. The distance form the earth

    d. None of the above

29. Terrestrial planets are

    a. Made of rock

    b. Have people on them

    c. The earth and no others

    d. The same size as Earth

30. How many planets orbit the sun in less than 224.7 days?

    a. 1 planet

    b. Only Venus

    c. 2 planets

    d. 3 planets

Strategy 9 - Try Every Option

For definition questions, try out all the options - one option will fit better than the rest. As you go through the options, use Strategy 5 - Elimination, to eliminate obviously incorrect choices as you go.

Directions: Read the passage below, and answer the questions using this strategy.

On Earth, common weather phenomena include wind, cloud, rain, snow, fog and dust storms. Less common events include natural disasters such as tornadoes, hurricanes, typhoons and ice storms. Almost all weather phenomena occurs in the troposphere (the lower part of the atmosphere). Weather does occur in the stratosphere and can affect weather lower down in the troposphere, but the exact mechanisms are poorly understood.

Weather occurs primarily due to different temperature and moisture densities. The strong temperature contrast between polar and tropical air gives rise to the jet stream. Weather systems in the mid-latitudes, such as extra-tropical cyclones, are caused by instabilities of the jet stream flow. Weather systems in the tropics, such as monsoons or thunderstorms, are caused by different processes.

Because the Earth's axis is tilted relative to its orbital plane, sunlight is incident at different angles at different times of the year. In June the Northern Hemisphere is tilted towards the sun, so at any given Northern Hemisphere latitude, sunlight is more direct than in December. This effect causes seasons. Over thousands to hundreds of thousands of years, changes in Earth's orbital parameters affect the amount and distribution of solar energy received by the Earth and influence long-term climate. [2]

31. The troposphere is

    a. The highest strata of the atmosphere
    b. The lowest strata of the atmosphere
    c. The middle level of the atmosphere
    d. Not part of the atmosphere

32. Monsoons are

    a. Caused by instabilities in the jet stream
    b. Caused by processes other than instabilities in the jet stream
    c. Part of the jet stream
    d. Cause the jet stream

33. Extra-tropical cyclones occur

  a. In the tropics

  b. In temperate zones

  c. In the gulf stream

  d. In mid-latitudes

34. Tilted means:

  a. Slanted

  b. Rotating

  c. Connected to

  d. Bent

Strategy 10 - Work for it

For questions about supporting details, work is the key. Review the passage to locate the right option. Never forget the choices that you are given are designed to confuse, and they may *seem* reasonable answers. However, if they are not mentioned in the text, they are "red herring" answers.

The best answer is the exact answer mentioned in the text.

Directions: Read the passage below, and answer the questions using this strategy.

Ebola is the common term for a group of viruses belonging to genus Ebola virus (EBOV), which is a part of the family Filoviridae, and for the disease that they cause, Ebola hemorrhagic fever. The virus is named after the Ebola River, where the first recognized outbreak of Ebola hemorrhagic fever occurred.

The viruses are characterized by long filaments, and have a shape similar to that of the Marburg virus, also in the family Filoviridae, and possessing similar disease symptoms. There are several species within the Ebola virus genus, which in turn have several specific strains or serotypes.

The Zaire virus is the type species, which is also the first discovered and the most lethal. Ebola is transmitted primarily through bodily fluids, and to a limited extent through skin. The virus interferes with the endothelial cells lining the interior surface of blood vessels and platelet cells. As the blood vessel walls become damaged and the platelets are unable to coagulate, patients succumb to hypovolemic shock.

Ebola first emerged in 1976 in Zaire. It remained largely obscure until 1989 with the outbreak in Reston, Virginia.[10]

35. The Ebola virus received this name because of

   a. The doctor who first discovered the virus

   b. The cure that is used to treat those infected

   c. The river where the disease was first encountered

   d. What the virus does to the body

36. Viruses in the Ebola genus are recognizable

   a. Because of their hooked shape

   b. Because of their long filaments

   c. Due to their oblong heads

   d. Because of their unique color

37. One of the most common causes of death from the Ebola family of viruses is

   a. Hypovolemic shock due to blood vessel damage

   b. Bleeding of the brain that cannot be stopped

   c. A heart attack from blood loss and lack of fluids

   d. A high fever that cannot be lowered

38. The most deadly strain of the Ebola virus family is the

   a. The Reston strain

   b. The Ivory Coast strain

   c. The Zaire strain

   d. The Sudan strain

Strategy 11 - Look at the Big Picture

Details can be tricky when dealing with main idea and summary questions, bu t do not let the details distract you. Look at the big picture instead of the smaller parts to determine the right answer.

Directions: Read the passage below, and answer the questions using this strategy.

As of late 2005, three fruit bat species have been identified as carrying the Ebola virus but not showing disease symptoms. They are now believed to be a natural host species, or reservoir, of the virus. Plants, arthropods, and birds have also been considered as reservoirs; however, bats are considered the most likely candidate.

Bats were known to reside in the cotton factory where the first outbreaks in 1976 and 1979 occurred, and they have also been implicated in Marburg infections in 1975 and 1980. Of 24 plant species and 19 vertebrate species experimentally inoculated with Ebola virus, only bats became infected. The absence of clinical signs in these bats is characteristic of a reservoir species.

In 2002-03, a survey of 1,030 animals from Gabon and the Republic of the Congo including 679 bats found Ebola virus RNA in 13 fruit bats (Hypsignathus monstrosus, Epomops franquetti and Myonycteris torquata). Bats are also known to be the reservoirs for several related viruses including Nipah virus, Hendra virus and Lyssa viruses.[11]

39. The species most suspected as a potential Ebola virus reservoir is

    a. Birds

    b. Insects

    c. Plants

    d. Bats

40. Most plant and animal species

a. Can carry the Ebola virus but not become infected

b. Can not carry and transmit the Ebola virus

c. Are responsible for new cases of Ebola viruses

d. Can be infected with one of the Ebola viruses

41. Bats are known for

a. Being carriers of many different viruses, including Ebola

b. Transmitting the Ebola virus through a scratch

c. Being susceptible to the virus and becoming infected

d. Transmitting the Ebola virus through infected droppings

Strategy 12 - Best Possible Answer

Try to determine the best possible answer according to the information given in the passage. Do not be distracted by answers that seem correct or are mostly correct.

Directions: Read the passage below, and answer the questions using this strategy.

In the early stages, Ebola may not be highly contagious. Contact with someone in early stages may not even transmit the disease. As the illness progresses, bodily fluids represent an extreme biohazard.

Due to lack of proper equipment and hygienic practices, large-scale epidemics occur mostly in poor, isolated areas without modern hospitals or well-educated medical staff. Many areas where the infectious reservoir exists have just these characteristics.

In such environments, all that can be done is immediately cease all needle sharing or use without adequate sterilization procedures, to isolate patients, and to observe strict barrier nursing procedures with the use of a medical-rated disposable face mask, gloves, goggles, and a gown always. This should be strictly enforced for all medical personnel and visitors. [10]

42. Ebola is highly contagious

a. Only when blood is present

b. Only in the first stages before hemorrhaging occurs

c. At all stages of the illness from incubation to recovery

d. Only in the later stages when the virus is very numerous

43. Exposure to the Ebola virus means

a. A death sentence for most patients

b. Isolation for the patient, and proper precautions for all medical personnel to contain the virus

c. The virus will spread rapidly and there is no treatment available

d. A full recovery usually, with very few symptoms

44. Ebola outbreaks commonly occur

a. Because sterilization and containment procedures are not followed or available

b. Due to infected animals in the area

c. Because of rat droppings in homes

d. Because of a contaminated water supply

45. Ebola is

a. More common in advanced nations where treatment makes the disease minor

b. More common in third world and developing countries

c. Fatal in more than ninety-five percent of the cases

d. Highly contagious during the incubation period

Answers to Sample Multiple-Choice Strategy Questions

Strategy 1 - Keywords in the question tells what the question is asking

1. B

The question asks about the free range *method* of farming. Here method refers to *type* of farming. "Method" here is the keyword and can be marked or underlined.

2. D

The Question is, "Free-range farming is *practiced* ..." The keyword here is "practiced." Looking at the choices, which all start with "to," it is clear the answer will be about *why* free range ... Also notice that one choice is "All of the above," which here, is the correct answer. However, when "All of the above" is an option, this is a potential Elimination strategy. All you have to do is find one option that is incorrect and you can use Strategy 5 - Elimination to eliminate two choices and increase your odds from one in four, to one in two.

3. A

The question is, "Free range farming husbandry ..." From the question, and the *lack* of keywords, together with the choices presented, the answer will be a definition free range farming husbandry.

4. C

The question is, "Free-range certification is *most important* to farmers because ... " The keywords here are "most important." Be careful to choose the best possible answer.

Strategy 2 - Negatives.

These four questions all have negatives: does not mean, is never, do not, and is not. These questions exclude possibilities, so if you see any choices that are true, you can eliminate them right away.

5. D

The question asks what sexual dimorphism does *not* mean. Circle the word "not" and keep it firmly in mind. Next, what is sexual dimorphism. Reading the text quickly, sexual dimorphism is not defined explicitly, but related to the female bears being smaller than the males. Probably there are other aspects, but this general definition is all that is needed to answer the question.

First, notice that "All of the above" is choice D. In addition the question is a negative. So in order for choice D to be correct, choices A, B and C must be *incorrect*. This narrows down your options. If any of choices A, B or C are correct, then you can eliminate that choice as well as choice D.

Either all the choices are *in*correct, in which case, choice D, "All of the above" is correct.

Choice A, male and females are the same size is incorrect. Choice B, all grizzly bears look the same and are the same size, is incorrect. Choice C, grizzly bears (plural so *all* grizzly bears) can be large and weigh more than half a ton. This is incorrect since while all grizzly bears are large, female bears weight less than half a ton.

All three choices are incorrect so choice D is the correct answer, "All of the Above," are incorrect.

6. A

First, circle or underline never to show this is a negative question. Now look at the options to find an option that is not true.

Choice A is true as male bears are 1,000 pounds. Place a mark beside this one. It may be tempting to select this option as your answer, but it is important to look at all choices before making a final decision.

Choice B is not true - size does not depend on the sex.
Choice C is not true - size does not depend on diet.
Choice D is not true - males often stand 8 feet.

So choice A is correct.

7. A

First circle "do not" to mark this as a negative question.

Choice A is correct, Yukon River grizzly bears do not get as big as other grizzlies, so put a mark beside it for later consideration. Examine the other choices before making a final decision.

Choice B is not mentioned in the text, and can be eliminated.

Choice C is not mentioned in the text and can be eliminated.

Choice D is true, but this is a negative question so it is false.

Some of the above choices may be true from a common sense point of view, but if they aren't mentioned specifically in the passage, they can be eliminated.

Choice A is correct.

Strategy 3 - Read the stem completely.

Read the question, and then look for the answer in the text before reading the choices. Reading the choices first will confuse, just as it is meant to do! Do not fall into this trap!

8. B

The choices here are very confusing and are meant to be! Four variations on the latin species name, Ursus Arctos are given, so the question is what version of this latin name is correct, which gives a very straight-forward strategy to solving. Since the name is latin, it is going to stand out in the text. Take the first option, "Arctas Ursinas," and scan the text for something that looks like that. At the end of the second sentence is "Ursus Arctos," which is very close. Next confirm what this sentence refers to, which gives the correct answer, Choice B.

9. D

This question asks why Kodiak brown bears are a different subspecies, and the options are designed to confuse a careless, stressed test-taker. Scan the text for "Kodiak," which appears in the second to last sentence, and answers the question.

10. C
This question asks about the relationship between brown bears and grizzly bears. If you are not careful you will be confused by the choices.

11. A
Read the question, then read the text before trying to answer and avoid confusion.

Strategy 4 - Consider all choices before deciding.

In Strategy 3, we learned to find the correct answer in the text before reading the choices. OK, now you have read the text and have the right answer. The next thing is Strategy 4 - Read *all* of the choices. Once you have read all of the choices, select the correct choice.

12. D
First, notice that "All of the above" is a choice. So if you find one option that is incorrect, you can eliminate that option and option D, "All of the above." Reading the question first, (Strategy #3) then looking in the text, and then reading all of the choices before answering, you can see that choices A, B and C are all correct, so choice D, All of the Above, is the correct choice.
If you had not read all the choices first, then you might be tempted to impulsively choose A, B, or C.

13. C
Looking at the choices, they are designed to confuse with different choices and combinations. Recognizing this, it is therefore important to be extra careful in making your choice. If you are stressed, in a hurry, or not paying attention, you will probably get this question wrong by making an impulsive choice and not reading through all the choices before making a selection.

Referring to the text, you will find the sentence, ."... it was a hybrid, with the mother a polar bear and the father a grizzly," which answers the question.

14. D
Reading through all the choices, B and C can be eliminated

right away as they are not referred to in the text. They might appear as good answers but they are not from the passage.

Looking at choices A and D, the issue is if this has happened before, or has it happened only in zoos. Referring to the text, the last sentence tells us the answer, "It is the first documented case in the wild, though it was known that this hybrid was biologically possible and other hybrids have been bred in zoos in the past."

15. B

Reading through the four choices, the question concerns, what does science know? Does it happen all the time? Completely understood? They do survive? Is it possible? Look in the text for how much is known. The last sentence, "It is the first documented case in the wild, though it was known that this hybrid was biologically possible" gives the answer.

Strategy 5 - Elimination.

For every question, no matter what type, eliminating obviously incorrect answers narrows the possible choices. Elimination is probably the most powerful strategy for answering multiple-choice.

16. A

Using this strategy the choices can be narrowed down to choices A and D. I have never seen a peacock with red in their tail, so choice C can *probably* be eliminated, but check back. Most birds and many animals have a pattern where the male is colorful and the female less colorful. Choice B can be eliminated as it refers to "both sexes" having colorful tails. Choice D is a good candidate as the text refers to molting season, however, the text does not say how long this is, so there is some doubt. This makes choice A the best choice as it is referred to directly in the text.

17. B

Choice D can be eliminated right away, as it is rare for a male bird to sit on eggs.

Skimming the passage, choices A and C can be eliminated, as they are not mentioned directly in the text, leaving only choice D.

18. C
Choices A and D can be eliminated right away, since "cock" always refers to a male bird. Referring to the text, "The male peafowl, or peacock, has long been ..." making choice C the best choice.

19. D
Choices A and B can be eliminated either right away or with a quick check of the passage, since they are not mentioned. Choice C is suspicious since the grey feathers are under the tail feathers, so it is difficult to see how they could be visible when the tail feathers are lowered.

Strategy 6 - Opposites

If there are opposites, one of them is generally the correct answer. If it helps, make a table that lays out the different options and the correct option will become clear.

20. D
Notice that choices A and D are opposites. Referring to the text, "Smallpox is an infectious disease unique to humans ..." eliminates choice A. Also notice choices B and C are not mentioned in the text and can be eliminated right away.

21. C
Notice that all the choices are opposites. 30 - 35% mortality, or survival rate, or 60%. Therefore, the task is to review the text, looking for 30% or 60%, survival or mortality, stay clear, and do not get confused. Sometimes making notes or a table can help to clarify.

The question is asking about percent, so it is easy and fast to skim the passage for a percent sign.

The first percent sign is in the second paragraph, 30 - 35%. Write this in the margin. Next, see what this percent refers to, which is the mortality rate. Write "mortality" next to 30 - 35%. Now, working backwards, see what the 30 - 35% mortality rate refers to. At the beginning of that sentence, is Variola Major.

30 - 35%	Mortality	V. Major

Now we have a clear understanding of what the passage is saying, which we have retrieved quickly and easily, and now hopefully we will not get confused by the different choices.

Choices A and B can be eliminated right away. Choice C looks correct. Check choice D quickly, and confirm that it is incorrect. Choice C is the correct answer.

22. B

Choices A and B are opposites. Is Variola Minor more or less severe, with more or fewer pox, and more or less scarring? The other two choices, "no pox" and "no treatment" can be eliminated quickly. Either choice A or B are going to be wrong.

Make a quick table like this:

Major - more serious - scars, blindness
Minor - milder

The passage does not mention scarring from Variola minor, but we can infer that it is milder. Looking at the options, choice A is clearly talking about Variola major, and we can infer that choice B is talking about Variola minor and is the correct answer. We can confirm our inference from the text.

Also note the words, 'major' and 'minor.' Which gives a clue concerning severity, and the elimination of choice A.

23. A

Choices A and B are not exactly opposite, but very close and designed to confuse if you do not read them properly. How many people die from the virus? Between 30 and 35%? Or between 35 and 60%? Scan the text with these numbers in mind.

This question is asking about a percent figures, so quickly scan the passage for a percent sign, which first appears in the second paragraph. Working back, confirm that the percent figures is related to mortality, which it is.

Strategy 7 - Look for Differences.

Look at two choices that appear to be correct and examine them carefully.

24. B
Choices A, B and C are very similar and designed to confuse and distract someone who does not look carefully at the text. What is astraphobia exactly? This is a definition question for an unusual word, astraphobia. Scan the text for "astraphobia." Choice B is correct.

25. C
Choices A, B and C are similar and designed to confuse, or tempt a stressed or careless test-taker into making a quick and incorrect choice. Checking the passage, in the first paragraph, lightning occurs in thunderstorms, volcanic eruptions and in dust storms, so choice C is correct.

26. C
All four answers are similar and designed to confuse. Seeing how similar the choices are, it is very important to be clear on the exact definition. Scan the text quickly for the word "fulgurites." From the first paragraph, fulgurites are formed when lightning is ."... hot enough to fuse silica sand into glass channels ..." so the correct answer, and the option that answers the question best, is choice C, "Made of silica turned into glass."

Strategy 8 - Context clues.

Look at the sentences and the context to determine the best option. Sometimes, the answer may be located right in the passage or question.

27. B
You do not have to know the exact meaning - just enough to answer the question. The phrase is used in the passage, "After the Moon, it is the brightest natural object in the night sky, reaching an apparent magnitude of −4.6" where Venus is compared to the brightness of the moon, so the apparent magnitude must have something to do with brightness, which is enough information to answer the question. Notice also,

how the choices are opposites. Choice A and B are opposites as are choices C and D.

28. A
The exact meaning is not necessary, you only need only enough information to answer the question. The passage where this phrase is used is, "Because Venus is an inferior planet from Earth, it never appears to venture far from the Sun: its elongation reaches a maximum of 47.8°." Elongation in this sentence is something connected with distance from the sun, but also something to do with Earth. Choice C can be eliminated right away, and since one choice is wrong, Choice D, All of the Above, can also be eliminated. Choice A is the most likely correct because it mentions, "as seen from earth."

29. A
Choices C and D can be eliminated right away. No mention is made of size or people, so choices C and D are also incorrect. Terrestrial has many similar meanings, but choice A is the best. From the passage, "Venus is one of the four solar terrestrial planets, meaning that, like the Earth, it is a rocky body."

Note that choice B is a grammatical error and can be eliminated right away. The question is, "Terrestrial planets are," and choice B is, "Have people on them."

This is a great strategy, looking for grammatical errors and eliminating, and what you might expect to see on a test that a professor has made themselves. However, most standardized tests are generated by computer, and proofed by many different people who have considerable expertise in correcting this type of easy question. Keep this in mind because it is an easy elimination, but don't expect to see this type of thing on a standardized test.

30. A
This is a bit of a trick question and designed to confuse, as it requires an additional step of logical reasoning. Referring to the text, Venus is the *second* closest planet to the sun so there must be one planet that is closer. Planets closer to the sun will rotate the sun faster, so the answer must be choice A.

Strategy 9 - Try out every option for word meaning questions.

For definition questions, try out all the options - one option will fit better than the rest. As you go through the options, use Strategy 5 - Elimination, to eliminate obviously incorrect choices as you go.

31. B
The answer is taken directly from the passage. Notice that choices A and B are opposites, so one of them will be incorrect. Look in the text carefully for the exact definition. If you are uncertain, make a table in the margin.

Scan the passage looking for the word you are asked to define. Large or unusual words generally stand out and can be located quickly. Once you have found the position in the passage of the word using quick reading scanning techniques, then focus on the sentence and read carefully.

32. B
The sentences talking about the jet stream and monsoons are next to one another. Trying each definition, and comparing to the text, only choice B fits. If you are uncertain, copy the information from the passage into a table.

The question is, what is the relationship between monsoons and the jet stream.

Scan the passage for "jet stream" and "monsoon."

Tropical cyclones	Jet stream
Monsoons and thunderstorms	Different processes

33. D
Referring to the passage, and trying each definition choice, choice D is the only answer that makes sense referring to the text.

34. A
The passage from the text is, "Because the Earth's axis is tilted relative to its orbital plane, sunlight is incident at different angles at different times of the year." Substituting all the

choices given into this sentence, slanted, choice A, is the only sensible answer. Here is what substitutions look like:

> a. In June the Northern Hemisphere is *slanted* towards the sun...

> b. In June the Northern Hemisphere is *rotating* towards the sun...

> c. In June the Northern Hemisphere is *connected to* towards the sun...

> d. In June the Northern Hemisphere is *bent* towards the sun...

Choice A is the only one that makes sense.

Strategy 10 - You have to work for it! Check carefully for supporting details.

All answers can be found by carefully reading the text. The questions paraphrase the text found in the passage.

35. C
The passage has a lot of details so read carefully and stay clear.

36. B
The choices are designed to confuse. Check the text for the exact definition and do not be distracted by other choices.

37. A
Here is a quick tip. On choice A, the word hypovolemic is used. This is an unusual word and specific medical vocabulary. None of the other choices uses any specific vocabulary like this, so it is very likely to be the right answer. You can quickly scan the text for this word to confirm. Scanning the text for an unusual word is easy and fast, and one of the most powerful techniques for this type of question.

38. C
Scan the text for Zaire.

Strategy 11 - Look at the big picture

Details can be tricky when dealing with main idea and summary questions, but do not let the details distract you. Look at the big picture instead of the smaller parts to determine the right answer.

39. D
The passage says in 2005 it was found there are 3 fruit bat species most suspected of carrying the virus. The details (3 species, fruit bats and 2005) do not matter. Only the fact that bats are suspected.

40. B
The relevant passage is, "Of 24 plant species and 19 vertebrate species experimentally inoculated with Ebola virus, only bats became infected." The inference is that these plant and animal species cannot be infected, (i.e. carry and transmit the disease) so choice B is correct.

41. A
The relevant passage is, "Bats are also known to be the reservoirs for several related viruses including Nipah virus, Hendra virus and Lyssaviruses."

Strategy 12 - Make the best choice based on the information given.

42. D
Choices B and C are incorrect by the passage, "In the early stages, Ebola may not be highly contagious." Choice A is not mentioned, leaving choice D.

43. B
The passage does not say anything about the information in choices A and D. Choice C is irrelevant to the question.

44. A
Choices B and C are not mentioned in the passage. Choice D is a good possibility, however, choice A covers choice D and is referred to in the passage.

45. B
Choice A is incorrect. Choices C and D are not mentioned.

Practice Questions Answer Sheet

	A	B	C	D	E		A	B	C	D	E
1	○	○	○	○	○	21	○	○	○	○	○
2	○	○	○	○	○	22	○	○	○	○	○
3	○	○	○	○	○	23	○	○	○	○	○
4	○	○	○	○	○	24	○	○	○	○	○
5	○	○	○	○	○						
6	○	○	○	○	○						
7	○	○	○	○	○						
8	○	○	○	○	○						
9	○	○	○	○	○						
10	○	○	○	○	○						
11	○	○	○	○	○						
12	○	○	○	○	○						
13	○	○	○	○	○						
14	○	○	○	○	○						
15	○	○	○	○	○						
16	○	○	○	○	○						
17	○	○	○	○	○						
18	○	○	○	○	○						
19	○	○	○	○	○						
20	○	○	○	○	○						

Reading Comprehension Practice Questions

Questions 1 - 4 refer to the following passage.

Passage 1: "If You Have Allergies, You're Not Alone"

People who experience allergies might joke that their immune systems have let them down or are seriously lacking. Truthfully though, people who experience allergic reactions or allergy symptoms during certain times of the year have heightened immune systems that are, "better" than those of people who have perfectly healthy but less militant immune systems.

Still, when a person has an allergic reaction, they are having an adverse reaction to a substance that is considered normal to most people. Mild allergic reactions usually have symptoms like itching, runny nose, red eyes, or bumps or discoloration of the skin. More serious allergic reactions, such as those to animal and insect poisons or certain foods, may result in the closing of the throat, swelling of the eyes, low blood pressure, an inability to breathe, and can even be fatal.

Different treatments help different allergies, and which one a person uses depends on the nature and severity of the allergy. It is recommended to patients with severe allergies to take extra precautions, such as carrying an EpiPen, which treats anaphylactic shock and may prevent death, always in order for the remedy to be readily available and more effective. When an allergy is not so severe, treatments may be used just relieve a person of uncomfortable symptoms. Over the counter allergy medicines treat milder symptoms, and can be bought at any grocery store and used in moderation to help people with allergies live normally.

There are many tests available to assess whether a person has allergies or what they may be allergic to, and advances in these tests and the medicine used to treat patients continues to improve. Despite this fact, allergies still affect many people throughout the year or even every day. Medicines used to treat allergies have side effects of their own, and it is difficult to bring the body into balance with the use of medicine. Regardless, many of those who live with allergies are grateful for what is available and find it useful in maintaining their lifestyles.

1. According to this passage, it can be understood that the word "militant" belongs in a group with the words:

    a. sickly, ailing, faint

    b. strength, power, vigor

    c. active, fighting, warring

    d. worn, tired, breaking down

2. The author says that "medicines used to treat allergies have side effects of their own" to

    a. point out that doctors aren't very good at diagnosing and treating allergies

    b. argue that because of the large number of people with allergies, a cure will never be found

    c. explain that allergy medicines aren't cures and some compromise must be made

    d. argue that more wholesome remedies should be researched and medicines banned

3. It can be inferred that _____ recommend that some people with allergies carry medicine with them.

    a. the author

    b. doctors

    c. the makers of EpiPen

    d. people with allergies

4. The author has written this passage to

    a. inform readers on symptoms of allergies so people with allergies can get help

    b. persuade readers to be proud of having allergies

    c. inform readers on different remedies so people with allergies receive the right help

    d. describe different types of allergies, their symptoms, and their remedies

Questions 5 - 8 refer to the following passage.

Passage 2: "When a Poet Longs to Mourn, He Writes an Elegy"

Poems are an expressive, especially emotional, form of writing. They have been present in literature virtually from the time civilizations invented the written word. Poets often portrayed as moody, secluded, and even troubled, but this is because poets are introspective and feel deeply about the current events and cultural norms they are surrounded with. Poets often produce the most telling literature, giving insight into the society and mind-set they come from. This can be done in many forms.

The oldest types of poems often include many stanzas, may or may not rhyme, and are more about telling a story than experimenting with language or words. The most common types of ancient poetry are epics, which are usually extremely long stories that follow a hero through his journey, or elegies, which are often solemn in tone and used to mourn or lament something or someone. The Mesopotamians are often said to have invented the written word, and their literature is among the oldest in the world, including the epic poem titled "Epic of Gilgamesh." Similar in style and length to "Gilgamesh" is "Beowulf," an elegy poem written in Old English and set in Scandinavia. These poems are often used by professors as the earliest examples of literature.

The importance of poetry was revived in the Renaissance. At

this time, Europeans discovered the style and beauty of ancient Greek arts, and poetry was among those. Shakespeare is the most well-known poet of the time, and he used poetry not only to write poems but also to write plays for the theater. The most popular forms of poetry during the Renaissance included villanelles (a nineteen-line poem with two rhymes throughout), sonnets, as well as the epic. Poets during this time focused on style and form, and developed very specific rules and outlines for how an exceptional poem should be written.

As often happens in the arts, modern poets have rejected the constricting rules of Renaissance poets, and free form poems are much more popular. Some modern poems would read just like stories if they weren't arranged into lines and stanzas. It is difficult to tell which poems and poets will be the most important, because works of art often become more famous in hindsight, after the poet has died and society can look at itself without being in the moment. Modern poetry continues to develop, and will no doubt continue to change as values, thought, and writing continue to change.

Poems can be among the most enlightening and uplifting texts for a person to read if they are looking to connect with the past, connect with other people, or try to gain an understanding of what is happening in their time.

5. In summary, the author has written this passage

    a. as a foreword that will introduce a poem in a book or magazine

    b. because she loves poetry and wants more people to like it

    c. to give a brief history of poems

    d. to convince students to write poems

6. The author organizes the paragraphs mainly by

a. moving chronologically, explaining which types of poetry were common in that time

b. talking about new types of poems each paragraph and explaining them a little

c. focusing on one poet or group of people and the poems they wrote

d. explaining older types of poetry so she can talk about modern poetry

7. The author's claim that poetry has been around "virtually from the time civilizations invented the written word" is supported by the detail that

a. Beowulf is written in Old English, which is not really in use any longer

b. epic poems told stories about heroes

c. the Renaissance poets tried to copy Greek poets

d. the Mesopotamians are credited with both inventing the word and writing "Epic of Gilgamesh"

8. According to the passage, it can be understood that the word "telling" means

a. speaking

b. significant

c. soothing

d. wordy

Questions 9 - 12 refer to the following passage.

Passage 3: "Winged Victory of Samothrace: the Statue of the Gods"

Students who read about the "Winged Victory of Samothrace" probably won't be able to picture what this statue looks like. However, almost anyone who knows a little about statues will recognize it when they see it: it is the statue of a winged woman who does not have arms or a head. Even the most famous pieces of art may be recognized by sight but not by name.

This iconic statue is of the Greek goddess Nike, who represented victory and was called Victoria by the Romans. The statue is sometimes called the "Nike of Samothrace." She was often displayed in Greek art as driving a chariot, and her speed or efficiency with the chariot may be what her wings symbolize. It is said that the statue was created around 200 BCE to celebrate a battle that was won at sea. Archaeologists and art historians believe the statue may have originally been part of a temple or other building, even one of the most important temples, Megaloi Theoi, just as many statues were used during that time.

"Winged Victory" does indeed appear to have had arms and a head when it was originally created, and it is unclear why they were removed or lost. Indeed, they have never been discovered, even with all the excavation that has taken place. Many speculate that one of her arms was raised and put to her mouth, as though she was shouting or calling out, which is consistent with the idea of her as a war figure. If the missing pieces were ever to be found, they might give Greek and art historians more of an idea of what Nike represented or how the statue was used. Learning about pieces of art through details like these can help students remember time frames or locations, as well as learn about the people who occupied them.

9. The author's title says the statue is "of the Gods" because

> a. the statue is very beautiful and even a god would find it beautiful
>
> b. the statue is of a Greek goddess, and gods were of primary importance to the Greek
>
> c. Nike lead the gods into war
>
> d. the statues were used at the temple of the gods and so it belonged to them

10. The third paragraph states that

a. the statue is related to war and was probably broken apart by foreign soldiers

b. the arms and head of the statue cannot be found because all the excavation has taken place

c. speculations have been made about what the entire statue looked like and what it symbolized

d. the statue has no arms or head because the sculptor lost them

11. The author's main purpose in writing this passage is to

a. demonstrate that art and culture are related and one can teach us about the other

b. persuade readers to become archeologists and find the missing pieces of the statue

c. teach readers about the Greek goddess Nike

d. to teach readers the name of a statue they probably recognize

12. The author specifies the indirect audience as "students" because

a. it is probably a student who is taking this test

b. most young people don't know much about art yet and most young people are students

c. students read more than people who are not students

d. the passage is based on a discussion of what we can learn about culture from art

Questions 13 - 16 refer to the following passage.

Passage 4: "Ways Characters Communicate in Theater"

Playwrights give their characters voices in a way that gives depth and added meaning to what happens on stage during their play. There are different types of speech in scripts that allow characters to talk with themselves, with other characters, and even with the audience.

It is very unique to theater that characters may talk "to themselves." When characters do this, the speech they give is called a soliloquy. Soliloquies are usually poetic, introspective, moving, and can tell audience members about the feelings, motivations, or suspicions of an individual character without that character having to reveal them to other characters on stage. "To be or not to be" is a famous soliloquy given by Hamlet as he considers difficult but important themes, such as life and death.

The most common type of communication in plays is when one character is speaking to another or a group of other characters. This is generally called dialogue, but can also be called monologue if one character speaks without being interrupted for a long time. It is not necessarily the most important type of communication, but it is the most common because the plot of the play cannot really progress without it.

Lastly, and most unique to theater (although it has been used somewhat in film) is when a character speaks directly to the audience. This is called an aside, and scripts usually specifically direct actors to do this. Asides are usually comical, an inside joke between the character and the audience, and very short. The actor will usually face the audience when delivering them, even if it's for a moment, so the audience can recognize this move as an aside.

All three of these types of communication are important to the art of theater, and have been perfected by famous playwrights like Shakespeare. Understanding these types of communication can help an audience member grasp what is artful about the script and action of a play.

13. According to the passage, characters in plays communicate to

a. move the plot forward

b. show the private thoughts and feelings of one character

c. make the audience laugh

d. add beauty and artistry to the play

14. When Hamlet delivers "To be or not to be," he can most likely be described as

a. solitary

b. thoughtful

c. dramatic

d. hopeless

15. The author uses parentheses to punctuate "although it has been used somewhat in film"

a. to show that films are less important

b. instead of using commas so that the sentence is not interrupted

c. because parenthesis help separate details that are not as important

d. to show that films are not as artistic

16. It can be understood that by the phrase "give their characters voices," the author means that

a. playwrights are generous

b. playwrights are changing the sound or meaning of characters' voices to fit what they had in mind

c. dialogue is important in creating characters

d. playwrights may be the parent of one of their actors and literally give them their voice

Questions 17 - 20 refer to the following passage.

Passage 5: "Women and Advertising"

Only in the last few generations have media messages been so widespread and so readily seen, heard, and read by so many people. Advertising is an important part of both selling and buying anything from soap to cereal to jeans. For whatever reason, more consumers are women than are men. Media message are subtle but powerful, and more attention has been paid lately to how these message affect women.

Of all the products that women buy, makeup, clothes, and other stylistic or cosmetic products are among the most popular. This means that companies focus their advertising on women, promising them that their product will make her feel, look, or smell better than the next company's product will. This competition has resulted in advertising that is more and more ideal and less and less possible for everyday women. However, because women do look to these ideals and the products they represent as how they can potentially become, many women have developed unhealthy attitudes about themselves when they have failed to become those ideals.

In recent years, more companies have tried to change advertisements to be healthier for women. This includes featuring models of more sizes and addressing a huge outcry against unfair tools such as airbrushing and photo editing. There is debate about what the right balance between real and ideal is, because fashion is also considered art and some changes are made to purposefully elevate fashionable products and signify that they are creative, innovative, and the work of individual people. Artists want their freedom protected as much as women do, and advertising agencies are often caught in the middle.

Some claim that the companies who make these changes are not doing enough. Many people worry that there are still not enough models of different sizes and different ethnicities. Some people claim that companies use this healthier type of advertisement not for the good of women, but because they would like to sell products to the women who are looking for these kinds of messages. This is also a hard balance to find: companies do need to make money, and women do need to feel respected.

While the focus of this change has been on women, advertising can also affect men, and this change will hopefully be a lesson on media for all consumers.

17. The second paragraph states that advertising focuses on women

    a. to shape what the ideal should be

    b. because women buy makeup

    c. because women are easily persuaded

    d. because of the types of products that women buy

18. According to the passage, fashion artists and female consumers are at odds because

    a. there is a debate going on and disagreement drives people apart

    b. both of them are trying to protect their freedom to do something

    c. artists want to elevate their products above the reach of women

    d. women are creative, innovative, individual people

19. The author uses the phrase "for whatever reason" in this passage to

    a. keep the focus of the paragraph on media messages and not on the differences between men and women

    b. show that the reason for this is unimportant

    c. argue that it is stupid that more women are consumers than men

    d. show that he or she is tired of talking about why media messages are important

20. This passage suggests that

a. advertising companies are still working on making their messages better

b. all advertising companies seek to be more approachable for women

c. women are only buying from companies that respect them

d. artists could stop producing fashionable products if they feel bullied

Questions 21 - 24 refer to the following passage.

Passage 6: "FDR, the Treaty of Versailles, and the Fourteen Points"

At the conclusion of World War I, both who had won the war and those who were forced to admit defeat welcomed the end of the war and anticipated that a peace treaty would be signed. The American president, Franklin Roosevelt, played an important part in proposing what the agreements should be and did so through his Fourteen Points.

World War I had begun in 1914 when an Austrian archduke was assassinated, leading to a domino effect that pulled the world's most powerful countries into war on a large scale. The war catalyzed the creation and use of deadly weapons that had not previously existed, resulting in a great loss of soldiers on both sides of the fighting. More than 9 million soldiers were killed.

The United States agreed to enter the war right before it ended, and they believed that its decision to become finally involved brought on the end of the war. FDR made it very clear that the U.S. was entering the war for moral reasons and had an agenda focused on world peace. The Fourteen Points were individual goals and ideas (focused on peace, free trade, open communication, and self reliance) that FDR wanted the power nations to strive for now that the war had concluded.

He was optimistic and had many ideas about what could be accomplished through and during the post-war peace. However, FDR's fourteen points were poorly received when he presented them to the leaders of other world powers, many of whom wanted only to help their own countries and to punish the Germans for fueling the war, and they fell by the wayside. World War II was imminent, for Germany lost everything.

Some historians believe that the other leaders who participated in the Treaty of Versailles weren't receptive to the Fourteen Points because World War I was fought almost entirely on European soil, and the United States lost much less than did the other powers. FDR was in a unique position to help determine the fate of the war, but doing it on his own terms did not help accomplish his goals. This is only one historical example of how the United State has tried to use its power as an important country, but found itself limited because of geological or ideological factors.

21. The main idea of this passage is that

a. World War I was unfair because no fighting took place in America

b. World War II happened because of the Treaty of Versailles

c. the power the United States has to help other countries also prevents it from helping other countries

d. Franklin Roosevelt was one of the United States' smartest presidents

22. According to the second paragraph, World War I started because

a. an archduke was assassinated

b. weapons that were more deadly had been developed

c. a domino effect of allies agreeing to help

d. the world's most powerful countries were large

23. The author includes the detail that 9 million soldiers were killed

    a. to demonstrate why European leaders were hesitant to accept peace

    b. to show the reader the dangers of deadly weapons

    c. to make the reader think about which countries lost the most soldiers

    d. to demonstrate why World War II was imminent

24. According to this passage, it can be understood that the word catalyzed means

    a. analyzed

    b. sped up

    c. invented

    d. funded

Answer Key

Passage 1: "If You Have Allergies, You're Not Alone"

1. C

This question tests the reader's vocabulary skills. The uses of the negatives "but" and "less," especially right next to each other, may confuse readers into answering with choices A or D, which list words that are antonyms of "militant." Readers may also be confused by the comparison of healthy people with what is being described as an overly healthy person--both people are good, but the reader may look for which one is "worse" in the comparison, and therefore stray toward the antonyms. One key to understanding the meaning of "militant" if the reader is unfamiliar with it is to look at the root of the word; readers can then easily associate it with "military" and gain a sense of what the word signifies: defense (especially considered that the immune system defends the body). Choice C is correct over choice B because "militant" is an adjective, just as the words in C are, whereas the words in B are nouns.

2. C

This question tests the reader's understanding of function within writing. The other choices are details included surrounding the quoted text, and may therefore confuse the reader. A somewhat contradicts what is said earlier in the paragraph, which is that tests and treatments are improving, and probably doctors are along with them, but the paragraph doesn't actually mention doctors, and the subject of the question is the medicine. Choice B may seem correct to readers who aren't careful to understand that, while the author does mention the large number of people affected, the author is touching on the realities of living with allergies rather about the likelihood of curing all allergies. Similarly, while the author does mention the "balance" of the body, which is easily associated with "wholesome," the author is not really making an argument and especially is not making an extreme statement that allergy medicines should be outlawed. Again, because the article's tone is on living with allergies, choice C is an appropriate choice that fits with the title and content of the text.

3. B

This question tests the reader's inference skills. The text does not state who is doing the recommending, but the use of the "patients," as well as the general context of the passage, lends itself to the logical partner, "doctors," B. The author does mention the recommendation but doesn't present it as her own (i.e. "I recommend that"), so A may be eliminated. It may seem plausible that people with allergies (D) may recommend medicines or products to other people with allergies, but the text does not necessarily support this interaction taking place. Choice C may be selected because the EpiPen is specifically mentioned, but the use of the phrase "such as" when it is introduced is not limiting enough to assume the recommendation is coming from its creators.

4. D

This question tests the reader's global understanding of the text. Choice D includes the main topics of the three body paragraphs, and isn't too focused on a specific aspect or quote from the text, as the other questions are, giving a skewed summary of what the author intended. The reader may be drawn to Choice B because of the title of the passage and the use of words like "better," but the message of the passage is larger and more general than this.

Passage 2: "When a Poet Longs to Mourn, He Writes an Elegy"

5. C

This question tests the reader's summarization skills. The use of the word "actually" in describing what kind of people poets are, as well as other moments like this, may lead readers to selecting choice B or D, but the author is more information than trying to persuade readers. The author gives no indication that she loves poetry (B) or that people, students specifically (D), should write poems. Choice A is incorrect because the style and content of this paragraph do not match those of a foreword; forewords usually focus on the history or ideas of a specific poem to introduce it more fully and help it stand out against other poems. The author here focuses on several poems and gives broad statements. Instead, she tells a kind of story about poems, giving three very broad time periods in which to discuss them, thereby giving a brief history of poetry, as choice C states.

6. A
This question tests the reader's summarization skills. Key words in the topic sentences of each of the paragraphs ("oldest," "Renaissance," "modern") should give the reader an idea that the author is moving chronologically. The opening and closing sentence-paragraphs are broad and talk generally. Choice B seems reasonable, but epic poems are mentioned in two paragraphs, eliminating the idea that only new types of poems are used in each paragraph. Choice C is also easily eliminated because the author clearly mentions several different poets, groups of people, and poems. Choice D also seems reasonable, considering that the author does move from older forms of poetry to newer forms, but use of "so (that)" makes this statement false, for the author gives no indication that she is rushing (the paragraphs are about the same size) or that she prefers modern poetry.

7. D
This question tests the reader's attention to detail. The key word is "invented"--it ties together the Mesopotamians, who invented the written word, and the fact that they, as the inventors, also invented and used poetry. The other selections focus on other details mentioned in the passage, such as that the Renaissance's admiration of the Greeks (C) and that Beowulf is in Old English (A). Choice B may seem like an attractive answer because it is unlike the others and because the idea of heroes seems rooted in ancient and early civilizations.

8. B
This question tests the reader's vocabulary and contextualization skills. "Telling" is not an unusual word, but it may be used here in a way that is not familiar to readers, as an adjective rather than a verb in gerund form. Choice A may seem like the obvious answer to a reader looking for a verb to match the use they are familiar with. If the reader understands that the word is being used as an adjective and that choice A is a ploy, they may opt to select choice D, "wordy," but it does not make sense in context. Choice C can be easily eliminated, and doesn't have any connection to the paragraph or passage. "Significant" (B) does make sense contextually, especially relative to the phrase "give insight" used later in the sentence.

Passage 3: "Winged Victory of Samothrace: the Statue of the Gods"

9. B
This question tests the reader's summarization skills. Choice A is a very broad statement that may or may not be true, and seems to be in context, but has nothing to do with the passage. The author does mention that the statue was probably used on a temple dedicated to the Greek gods (D), but in no way discusses or argues for the gods' attitude toward or claim on these temples or its faucets. Nike does indeed lead the gods into a war (the Titan war), as choice C suggests, but this is not mentioned by the passage and students who know this may be drawn to this answer but have not done a close enough analysis of the text that is actually in the passage. Choice B is appropriately expository, and connects the titular emphasis to the idea that the Greek gods are very important to Greek culture.

10. C
This question tests the reader's summarization skills. The test for question choice C is pulled straight from the paragraph, but is not word-for-word, so it may seem too obvious to be the right answer. The passage does talk about Nike being the goddess of war, as choice A states, but the third paragraph only touches on it and it is an inference that soldiers destroyed the statue, when this question is asking specifically for what the third paragraph actually stated. Choice B is also straight from the text, with a minor but key change: the inclusion of the words "all" and "never" are too limiting and the passage does not suggest that these limits exist. If a reader selects choice D, they are also making an inference that is misguided for this type of question. The paragraph does state that the arms and head are "lost" but does not suggest who lost them.

11. A
This question tests the reader's ability to recognize function in writing. Choice B can be eliminated based on the purpose of the passage, which is expository and not persuasive. The author may or may not feel this way, but the passage does not show evidence of being argumentative for that purpose. Choices C and D are both details found in the text, but neither of them encompasses the entire message of the passage, which has an overall message of learning about culture from

art and making guesses about how the two are related, as suggested by choice A.

12. D
This question tests the reader's ability to understand function within writing. Most of the possible selections are very general statements which may or may not be true. It probably is a student who is taking the test on which this question is featured (A), but the author makes no address to the test taker and is not talking to the audience in terms of the test. Likewise, it may also be true that students read more than adults (C), mandated by schools and grades, but the focus on the verb "read" in the first sentence is too narrow and misses the larger purpose of the passage; the same could be said for selection B. While all the statements could be true, choice D is the most germane, and infers the purpose of the passage without making assumptions that could be incorrect.

Passage 4: "Ways Characters Communicate in Theater"

13. D
This question tests the reader's summarization skills. The question is asking very generally about the message of the passage, and the title, "Ways Characters Communicate in Theater," is one indication of that. The other choices A, B, and C are all directly from the text, and therefore readers may be inclined to select one of them, but are too specific to encapsulate the entirety of the passage and its message.

14. B
The paragraph on soliloquies mentions "To be or not to be," and it is from the context of that paragraph that readers may understand that because "To be or not to be" is a soliloquy, Hamlet will be introspective, or thoughtful, while delivering it. It is true that actors deliver soliloquies alone, and may be "solitary" (A), but "thoughtful" (B) is more true to the overall idea of the paragraph. Readers may choose C because drama and theater can be used interchangeably and the passage mentions that soliloquies are unique to theater (and therefore drama), but this answer is not specific enough to the paragraph in question. Readers may pick up on the theme of life and death and Hamlet's true intentions and select that he is "hopeless" (D), but those themes are not discussed either

by this paragraph or passage, as a close textual reading and
analysis confirms.

15. C
This question tests the reader's grammatical skills. Choice B
seems logical, but parenthesis are actually considered to be a
stronger break in a sentence than commas are, and along this
line of thinking, actually disrupt the sentence more. Choices
A and D make comparisons between theater and film that are
simply not made in the passage, and may or may not be true.
This detail does clarify the statement that asides are most
unique to theater by adding that it is not completely unique
to theater, which may have been why the author didn't chose
not to delete it and instead used parentheses to designate the
detail's importance (C).

16. C
This question tests the reader's vocabulary and contextualization skills. Choice A may or may not be true, but focuses
on the wrong function of the word "give" and ignores the rest
of the sentence, which is more relevant to what the passage
is discussing. CHoices B and D may also be selected if the
reader depends too literally on the word "give," failing to grasp
the more abstract function of the word that is the focus of
choice C, which also properly acknowledges the entirety of the
passage and its meaning.

Passage 5: "Women and Advertising"

17. D
This question tests the reader's summarization skills. The
other choices A, B, and C focus on portions of the second
paragraph that are too narrow and do not relate to the specific
portion of text in question. The complexity of the sentence
may mislead students into selecting one of these answers,
but rearranging or restating the sentence will lead the reader
to the correct answer. In addition, choice A makes an assumption that may or may not be true about the intentions
of the company, choice B focuses on one product rather than
the idea of the products, and choice C makes an assumption
about women that may or may not be true and is not supported by the text.

18. B
This question tests reader's attention to detail. If a reader selects A, he or she may have picked up on the use of the word "debate" and assumed, very logically, that the two are at odds because they are fighting; however, this is simply not supported in the text. Choice C also uses very specific quotes from the text, but it rearranges them and gives them false meaning. The artists want to elevate their creations above the creations of other artists, thereby showing that they are "creative" and "innovative." Similarly, choice D takes phrases straight from the texts and rearranges and confuses them. The artists are described as wanting to be "creative, innovative, individual people," not the women.

19. A
This question tests reader's vocabulary and summarization skills. This phrase, used by the author, may seem flippant and dismissive if readers focus on the word "whatever" and misinterpret it as a popular, colloquial terms. In this way, the choices B and C may mislead the reader to selecting one of them by including the terms "unimportant" and "stupid," respectively. Choice D is a similar misreading, but doesn't make sense when the phrase is at the beginning of the passage and the entire passage is on media messages. Choice A is literarily and contextually appropriate, and the reader can understand that the author would like to keep the introduction focused on the topic the passage is going to discuss.

20. A
This question tests a reader's inference skills. The extreme use of the word "all" in choice B suggests that every single advertising company are working to be approachable, and while this is not only unlikely, the text specifically states that "more" companies have done this, signifying that they have not all participated, even if it's a possibility that they may some day. The use of the limiting word "only" in choice C lends that answer similar problems; women are still buying from companies who do not care about this message, or those companies would not be in business, and the passage specifies that "many" women are worried about media messages, but not all. Readers may find choice D logical, especially if they are looking to make an inference, and while this may be a possibility, the passage does not suggest or discuss this

happening. Choice A is correct based on specifically because of the relation between "still working" in the answer and "will hopefully" and the extensive discussion on companies struggles, which come only with progress, in the text.

Passage 6: "FDR, the Treaty of Versailles, and the Fourteen Points"

21. C
This question tests the reader's summarization skills. The entire passage is leading up to the idea that the president of the US may not have had grounds to assert his Fourteen Points when other countries had lost so much. Choice A is pretty directly inferred by the text, but it does not adequately summarize what the entire passage is trying to communicate. Choice B may also be inferred by the passage when it says that the war is "imminent," but it does not represent the entire message, either. The passage does seem to be in praise of FDR, or at least in respect of him, but it does not in any way claim that he is the smartest president, nor does this represent the many other points included. Choice C is then the obvious answer, and most directly relates to the closing sentences which it rewords.

22. C
This question tests the reader's attention to detail. The passage does state that choices A and B are true, and while those statements are in proximity to the explanation for why the war started, they are not the actual reason given. Choice D is a mix up of words used in the passage, which says that the largest powers were in play but not that this fact somehow started the war. The passage does make a direct statement that a domino effect started the war, supporting choice C as the correct answer.

23. A
This question tests the reader's understanding of functions in writing. Throughout the passage, it states that leaders of other nations were hesitant to accept generous or peaceful terms because of the grievances of the war, and the great loss of life was chief among these. While the passage does touch on the devastation of deadly weapons (B), the use of this raw, emotional fact serves a much larger purpose, and the focus of the

passage is not the weapons. While readers may indeed consider who lost the most soldiers (C) when so many countries
were involved and the inequalities of loss are mentioned in the
passage, there is no discussion of this in the passage. Choice
D is related to A, but choice A is more direct and relates more
to the passage.

24. B
This question tests the reader's vocabulary skills. Choice A
may seem appealing to readers because it is phonetically
similar to "catalyzed," but the two are not related in any other
way. Choice C makes sense in context, but if plugged into
the sentence creates a redundancy that doesn't make sense.
Choice D does also not make sense contextually, even if the
reader may consider that funds were needed to create more
weaponry, especially if it was advanced.

Listening Comprehension Self-Assessment Answer Sheet

	A	B	C	D
1	○	○	○	○
2	○	○	○	○
3	○	○	○	○
4	○	○	○	○
5	○	○	○	○
6	○	○	○	○
7	○	○	○	○
8	○	○	○	○
9	○	○	○	○
10	○	○	○	○
11	○	○	○	○
12	○	○	○	○
13	○	○	○	○
14	○	○	○	○
15	○	○	○	○

Directions: Scan the QR code below with any smartphone or tablet for an audio recording of the listening comprehension passages below. Or, have someone read them to you. Listen carefully to the passages and answer the questions that follow.

What is a QR Code?
A QR code looks like a barcode and it's used as a shortcut to link to content online using your phone's camera, saving you from typing lengthy addresses into your mobile browser.

Questions 1 - 4 refer to the following passage.

Caterpillars

Butterfly larvae, or caterpillars, consume plant leaves and spend practically all their time in search of food. Although most caterpillars are herbivorous, a few species eat other insects. Some larvae form mutual associations with ants. They communicate with the ants using vibrations that are transmitted through the soil as well as using chemical signals. The ants provide some degree of protection to the larvae and they in turn gather honeydew secretions. [3]

Scan for audio

1. What do most larvae spend their time doing?

    a. Eating

    b. Sleeping

    c. Communicating with ants.

    d. None of the above

2. Are all caterpillars herbivores?

    a. Yes

    b. No, some eat insects

3. What benefit do larvae get from association with ants?

    a. They do not receive any benefit.

    b. Ants give them protection.

    c. Ants give them food.

    d. Ants give them honeydew secretions.

4. Do ants or larvae benefit most from association?

    a. Ants benefit most

    b. Larvae benefit most

    c. Both benefit the same

    d. Neither benefits

Questions 5 - 8 refer to the following passage.

Fire is the rapid oxidation of a material in the chemical process of combustion, releasing heat, light, and various reaction products. Fire is a rapid oxidization, unlike slower processes such as rust or digestion.
The flame is the visible portion of the fire. If hot enough, the gases may become ionized to produce plasma. Depending on the substances and impurities, the color of the flame and the fire's intensity varies.

Fire is an important process that affects ecological systems around the globe. The positive effects of fire include stimulating growth and maintaining various ecological systems. Fire has been used by humans for cooking, generating heat, light, signaling, and propulsion. The negative effects of fire include hazard to life and property, atmospheric pollution, and water contamination. If fire removes protective vegetation, heavy rainfall may lead to soil erosion. In addition, when vegetation is burned, the nitrogen it contains is released into the atmosphere, unlike elements such as potassium and phosphorus which remain in the ash and are quickly recycled into the soil. This loss of nitrogen caused by fire produces a long-term reduction in the fertility of the soil, which only recovers slowly as nitrogen is "fixed" from the atmosphere by lightning and by certain plants such as clover.

Fires starts when a flammable or a combustible material, in combination with a sufficient quantity of an oxidizer, such as oxygen gas, is exposed to a source of heat or ambient temperature above the flash point for the fuel/oxidizer mix, and is able to sustain a rate of rapid oxidation that produces a chain reaction. This is commonly called the fire tetrahedron. Fire cannot exist without all of these elements in place, and in the right proportions. For example, a flammable liquid will start burning only if the fuel and oxygen are in the right proportions. Some fuel-oxygen mixes may require a catalyst, a substance that is not consumed, but which enables the reactants to combust more readily.

Once ignited, a chain reaction must take place whereby fires can sustain its own heat by the further release of heat energy in the process of combustion and may propagate, provided there is a continuous supply of an oxidizer and fuel.

If the oxidizer is oxygen from the surrounding air, the presence of a force of gravity, or of some similar force caused by acceleration, is necessary to produce convection, which removes combustion products and brings a supply of oxygen to the fire. Without gravity, a fire rapidly surrounds itself with its own combustion products and non-oxidizing gases from the air, which exclude oxygen and extinguish the fire. Because of this, the risk of fire in a spacecraft is small when it is coasting in inertial flight. Of course, this does not apply if oxygen is supplied to the fire by some process other than thermal convection.

Fire can be extinguished by removing any one of the elements of the fire tetrahedron. Consider a natural gas flame, such as from a stovetop burner. The fire can be extinguished by any of the following:

- turning off the gas supply, which removes the fuel

source;

- covering the flame completely, which smothers the flame as the combustion both uses the available oxidizer (the oxygen in the air) and displaces it from the area around the flame with CO_2;

- application of water, which removes heat from the fire faster than the fire can produce it

- application of a retardant chemical such as Halon to the flame, which retards the chemical reaction itself until the rate of combustion is too slow to maintain the chain reaction.

In contrast, fire is intensified by increasing the overall rate of combustion. Methods to do this include increasing fuel and oxidizer input in this balanced mix, increasing the ambient temperature so the fire's own heat is better able to sustain combustion, or providing a catalyst; a non-reactant medium in which the fuel and oxidizer can more readily react.

Scan for audio

5. Are oxidation processes like rust the same as fire?

    a. Yes
    b. No

6. What causes flames to have different colors?

    a. The material burning and impurities

    b. The material burning

    c. Impurities in the surrounding air

    d. None of the above.

7. What is one of the positive effects of fire on ecological systems?

a. Fire stimulates grown and maintains some ecological systems

b. There are no beneficial effects on eco systems

c. Fire can stimulate grown but overall are not beneficial for ecosystems

d. None of the above

8. What happens to potassium and phosphorus when vegetation is burned?

a. Potassium and phosphorus are released into the atmosphere

b. Potassium and phosphorus are not involved in the burning of vegetation

c. Potassium and phosphorus remain in the ash

d. None of the above

Questions 9 – 13 refer to the following passage.

Fire Extinguishers

A fire extinguisher is an active fire protection device used to extinguish or control small fires, often in emergency situations. They are not intended for out-of-control fires, such as a fire that has reached the ceiling or endangers the user. Typically, a fire extinguisher consists of a hand-held cylindrical pressure vessel containing an agent which can be discharged to extinguish a fire.

In the United States, fire extinguishers in all buildings other than houses are generally required to be serviced and inspected by a Fire Protection service company at least annually. Some jurisdictions require more frequent service for fire extinguishers. The servicer places a tag on the extinguisher to show the type of service performed, such as annual inspection, recharge or replacement.

There are two main types of fire extinguishers: stored pressure and cartridge-operated. In stored pressure units, the expellant is stored in the same chamber as the fire fighting agent itself. Depending on the agent used, different propellants are used. With dry chemical extinguishers, nitrogen is typically used; water and foam extinguishers typically use air.

Stored pressure fire extinguishers are the most common type. Cartridge-operated extinguishers contain the expellant gas in a separate cartridge that is punctured before discharge, exposing the propellant to the extinguishing agent. This type is not as common, used primarily in areas such as industrial facilities, where they receive higher-than-average use. They have the advantage of simple and prompt recharge, allowing an operator to discharge the extinguisher, recharge it, and return to the fire in a reasonable amount of time. Unlike stored pressure types, these extinguishers use compressed carbon dioxide instead of nitrogen, although nitrogen cartridges are used on low temperature models. Cartridge operated extinguishers are available in dry chemical and dry powder types in the U.S.

Fire extinguishers are further divided into handheld and cart-mounted, also called wheeled extinguishers. Handheld extinguishers weigh from anywhere from 1 to 30 lbs. Cart-mounted units typically weigh more than 50 lbs. These wheeled models are most commonly found at construction sites, airport runways, heliports, as well as docks and marinas.

Scan for Audio

9. What types of fires are extinguishers NOT intended for?

    a. Electrical fires

    b. Out of control fires

    c. Fires on a boat or marina

    d. None of the above

10. How often are fire extinguishers inspected?

    a. Every 6 months

    b. There is no set time

    c. Every year

    d. Every 5 years

11. What are the two types of fire extinguishers?

    a. Stored pressure and cartridge-operated

    b. Chemical and water based

    c. Chemical and gas such as CO_2

    d. None of the above

12. What are two types of propellants used?

    a. Water and air

    b. Nitrogen and air

    c. Water and foam

    d. Chemical and dry

13. About how much do hand-held fire extinguishers weigh?

    a. 20 pounds

    b. 1 - 30 pounds

    c. 10 pounds

    d. 50 pounds

Questions 14 – 18 refer to the following passage.

Flame

A flame is a mixture of reacting gases and solids emitting visible, infrared, and sometimes ultraviolet light, depending on the chemical composition of the fuel. In many cases, such as the burning of organic matter like wood, or the incomplete combustion of gas, incandescent particles called soot produce the familiar red-orange glow of 'fire.' Complete combustion of gas has a dim blue color due to the emission of single-wavelength radiation formed in the flame. Usually oxygen is involved, but hydrogen burning in chlorine also produces a flame as well as other combinations.

Much of the radiation is emitted in the visible and infrared bands. The color depends on temperature and chemical make-up. The dominant color in a flame changes with temperature. Most flames have distinct zones which are different colors. At the bottom of the flame, where most burning is occurs, the fire is white, the hottest color possible for organic material, or yellow. Above the yellow region, the color changes to orange, which is cooler, then red, which is cooler still. Above the red region, combustion no longer occurs, and un-combusted carbon particles are visible as black smoke.
In combustion engines, various steps are taken to eliminate a flame. The method depends mainly on whether the fuel is oil, wood, or a high-energy fuel such as jet fuel.

Scan for audio

14. Does a flame omit ultraviolet light?

    a. Yes

    b. No

    c. Sometimes

15. Under what conditions is a flame orange-red?

a. Flames are always orange red

b. Flames are orange red when burning non-organic matter

c. Burning organic matter and the incomplete combustion of gas

d. None of the above

16. When are flames blue?

a. When the gases are not completely combusted

b. When the gases are complete combusted

c. When burning non-organic matter

d. None of the above

17. Is oxygen always present for a flame to burn?

a. Yes

b. No

18. What color is the flame in combustion engines?

a. Red

b. Orange

c. White

d. There is no flame in combustion engines

Questions 19 – 22 refer to the following passage.

Gardens

Ancient Roman gardens are known for their statues and sculptures, which were never missing from the lives of Romans. Romans designed their gardens with hedges and vines as well as a wide variety of flowers. Flowerbeds were very popular in the courtyards of the rich Romans.

The Middle Ages was a period of decline in gardening. After the fall of Rome, gardening was only for the purpose of growing medicinal herbs and decorating church altars.

Islamic gardens were built after the model of Persian gardens; enclosed by walls and divided in four by watercourses. Commonly, the center of the garden would have a pool or pavilion. Mosaics and glazed tiles used to decorate elaborate fountains are specific to Islamic gardens.[12]

Scan for audio

19. What is a characteristic feature of Roman gardens?

    a. Statues and Sculptures

    b. Flower beds

    c. Medicinal Herbs

    d. Courtyard gardens

20. When did gardening decline?

    a. Before the Fall of Rome.

    b. Gardening did not decline.

    c. Before the Middle Ages.

    d. After the Fall of Rome.

21. What kind of gardening was done during the Middle Ages?

    a. Gardening with hedges and vines

    b. Gardening with a wide variety of flowers

    c. Gardening for herbs and church alters

    d. Gardening divided by watercourses

22. What is a characteristic feature of Islamic Gardens?

   a. Statues and Sculptures

   b. Decorative tiles and fountains.

   c. Herbs

   d. Flower beds

Questions 23 – 24 refer to the following passage.

Insect Pests

Humans regard certain insects as pests and attempt to control them with insecticides and many other techniques. Some insects damage crops by feeding on sap, leaves or fruits, a few bite humans and livestock, alive and dead, to feed on blood. Some are capable of transmitting diseases to humans, pets and livestock. Many other insects are considered ecologically beneficial and a few provide direct economic benefit. Silkworms and bees have been domesticated for the production of silk and honey, respectively. [13]

Scan for audio

23. How do humans control insects?

   a. By training them

   b. Using insecticides and other techniques

   c. In many different ways

   d. Humans don't control insects

24. What are examples of beneficial insects?

    a. Cows and bats

    b. Bees and silkworms

    c. Caterpillars and ants

    d. None of the above

Questions 25 - 29 refer to the following passage.

Insects

Insects typically move by walking, flying and occasionally
swimming. Many insects walk with their legs touching
the ground in alternating triangles as this allows rapid,
yet stable movement. Insects are the only invertebrates
that can fly. Many insects spend at least part of their life
underwater. The larva stage has adapted gills. Some adult
insects live underwater and are excellent swimmers. Some
species, like water striders, are capable of walking on the
surface of water. Insects are mostly solitary, but some
insects, such as bees, ants, and termites, are social, and live
in large, well-organized colonies. Some insects, like earwigs,
care for their young, guarding their eggs and young. Insects
communicate with each other in a variety of ways. Many
species communicate with sounds: crickets stridulate, or rub
their wings together, often to attract a mate and drive off other
males. [13]

Scan for audio

25. Choose the correct sentence.

    a. Other invertebrates can fly.

    b. No other invertebrates can fly.

    c. Some other invertebrates can fly.

    d. Many other invertebrates can fly.

26. Choose the correct sentence.

    a. No insects can swim.

    b. All insects are excellent swimmers.

    c. Some insects are excellent swimmers.

    d. Most insects are excellent swimmers.

27. Choose the correct sentence.

    a. All insects communicate with sound.

    b. No insects communicate with sound.

    c. Insects don't communicate

    d. Many insects communicate with sound.

28. Insects use their wings to:

    a. Attract a mate and drive off males.

    b. Attract a mate and drive off females.

    c. Attract females and drive off mates.

    d. Attract males and drive off mates.

29. Are insects solitary or social?

    a. Solitary

    b. Social

    c. Some are social and some are solitary

    d. None of the above

Questions 30 - 34 refer to the following passage.

Trees

Trees are an important part of the natural landscape because they prevent erosion and protect ecosystems in, and under their branches. Trees also play an important role in producing oxygen and reducing carbon dioxide in the atmosphere, as well as moderating ground temperatures. Trees are important elements in landscaping and agriculture, both for their visual appeal and for their crops, such as apples. Wood from trees is a building material, and a primary energy source in many developing countries. Trees also play a role in many of the world's mythologies. [15]

30. What are two reasons trees are important in the natural landscape?

    a. They prevent erosion and produce oxygen.

    b. They produce fruit and are important elements in c. landscaping.

    c. Trees are not important in the natural landscape.

    d. Trees produce carbon dioxide and prevent erosion.

31. What kind of eco-systems do trees protect?

    a. Trees don't protect eco-systems.

    b. Weather sheltered eco-systems.

    c. Eco-systems around their base.

    d. All of the above.

32. Which of the following is true?

a. Trees provide a primary food source in the developing world.

b. Trees provide a primary building material in the developing world.

c. Trees provide a primary energy source in the developing world.

d. Trees provide a primary oxygen source in the developing world.

33. Why are trees important for agriculture?

a. Because of their crops.

b. Because they shelter eco-systems.

c. Because they are a source of energy.

d. Because of their visual appeal.

34. What do trees do to the atmosphere?

a. Trees produce carbon dioxide and reduce oxygen.

b. Trees produce oxygen and carbon dioxide.

c. Trees reduce oxygen and carbon dioxide.

d. Trees produce oxygen and reduce carbon dioxide.

Questions 35 - 37 refer to the following passage.

Trees II

With an estimated 100,000 species, trees represent 25 percent of all living plant species. The majority of tree species grow in tropical regions of the world and many of these areas have not been surveyed by botanists, making species diversity poorly understood. The earliest trees were tree ferns and horsetails, which grew in forests in the Carboniferous period. Tree ferns still survive, but the surviving horsetails are no longer in tree form. Later, in the Triassic period, conifers and ginkgos, appeared, followed by flowering plants in the Creta-ceous period. [15]

Scan for Audio

35. Do Botanists understand the number of tree species?

a. Yes botanists know exactly how many tree species there are.

b. No, species diversity is not well understood.

c. Yes, botanists are pretty sure.

d. No, botanist have no idea.

36. Where do most trees species grow?

a. Most tree species grow in tropical regions.

b. There is no one area where most tree species grow.

c. Tree species grow in 25% of the world.

d. There are 100,000 tree species.

37. What tree(s) survived from the Carboniferous period?

a. 25% of all trees

b. Horsetails

c. Conifers

d. Tree Ferns

Questions 38 - 40 refer to the following passage.

Wildfires

A wildfire is an uncontrolled fire, usually in a wilderness region. Other names such as brush fire, bush fire, forest fire, desert fire, grass fire, hill fire, peat fire and vegetation fire are used to describe the same phenomenon depending on the type of vegetation burned, and the regional variant of English.

A wildfire differs from other fires due to its extensive size, the speed it spreads, its potential to change direction unexpectedly, and the ability to jump gaps such as roads, rivers and fire breaks.

Wildfires are a common occurrence in Australia because of the generally hot and dry climate. They pose a great risk to life and infrastructure all times of the year, though mostly throughout the hotter months of summer and spring. Wildfires can cause extensive damage to property and human life, but they also have various beneficial effects on wilderness areas. Some plant species depend on the effects of fire for growth and reproduction, although large wildfires may also have negative ecological effects.

Strategies of wildfire prevention, detection, and suppression have varied over the years. One of the more controversial techniques is controlled burning. This involves permitting or even igniting smaller fires to minimize the amount of flammable material available for a potential wildfire. While some wildfires burn in remote forested regions, they can cause extensive destruction of homes and other property located in the wildland-urban interface: a zone of transition between developed areas and undeveloped wilderness.

The name wildfire was once a synonym for Greek fire but now refers to any large or destructive conflagration. Wildfires differ from other fires in that they take place outdoors in areas of grassland, woodlands, bushland, scrubland, peatland, and other wooded areas that act as a source of fuel. While the causes of wildfires vary and the outcomes are always unique, all wildfires can be characterized in terms of their physical properties, fuel type, and the effect of weather. Wildfire behavior and severity result from the combination of factors such as available fuels, physical setting, and weather. While wildfires can be large, uncontrolled disasters that burn through hundreds of square kilometers, they can also be as small as a fraction of one square kilometer.

Scan for audio

38. Why are their different names for wildfires?

a. The different names depend on the type of vegetation

b. The different names depend on the vegetation and the local English dialect

c. The different names depend on the local English dialect

d. The different names depend on their size

39. How are wildfires different form other fires?

a. Wildfires consume different types of vegetation and burn hotter

b. Wildfires only occur in dry climates

c. Wildfires are different because of their size and speed

d. Wildfires are different because they occur in wilderness areas

40. Why are wildfires common in Australia?

a. Due to the availability of vegetation

b. Due to the higher percentage of oxygen in the air

c. Due to the hot dry climate

d. None of the above

Answer Key

1. A
Eating. Larvae spend most of their time in search of food and their food is leaves.

2. B
Some caterpillars eat other insects.

3. B
From the passage, the ants provide some degree of protection

4. C
The association is mutual so they both benefit.

5. B
Fire is an oxidation process but is much faster than rust or digestion.

6. A
Depending on the substances, and impurities, the color of the flame and the fire's intensity will vary.

7. A
Fire stimulates grown and maintains some ecological systems.

8. C
In a fire, potassium and phosphorus remain in the ash.

9. B
Fire extinguishers are typically used for small fires and not intended for out-of-control fires, such as one which has reached the ceiling, or endangers the user.

10. C
Fire extinguishers are typically inspected every year, although some jurisdictions require more frequent inspections.

11. A
The two most common types of fire extinguishers are stored pressure and cartridge-operated.

12. B
With dry chemical extinguishers, nitrogen is typically used; water and foam extinguishers typically use air.

13. A
Hand-held fire extinguishers weigh between 1 and 30 pounds.

14. A
Solids emitting visible, infrared, and sometimes ultraviolet light, depending on the chemical composition of the fuel and reaction products

15. C
The burning of organic matter like wood, or the incomplete combustion of gas, incandescent solid particles called soot produce the familiar red-orange glow of 'fire.'

16. B
Complete combustion of gas has a dim blue color due to the emission of single-wavelength radiation from various electron transitions in the excited molecules formed in the flame.

17. A
Usually oxygen is involved, but hydrogen burning in chlorine also produces a flame, producing hydrogen chloride (HCl). Other possible combinations producing flames, amongst many, are fluorine and hydrogen, and hydrazine and nitrogen tetroxide.

18. D
There is no flame in combustion engines.

19. A
The ancient Roman gardens are known by their statues and sculptures.

20. D
After the fall of Rome, gardening was only for medicinal purposes, AND gardening declined in the Middle Ages, so we can infer gardening declined after the fall of Rome.

21. C
From the passage, "After the fall of Rome gardening was

only done with the purpose of growing medicinal herbs and decorating church altars."

22. B
From the passage, "Mosaics and glazed tiles used to decorate elaborate fountains are specific to Islamic gardens."

23. B
The techniques for controlling insects is taken directly from the first sentence.

24. B
Bees and silkworms are examples of beneficial insects.

25. B
From the passage, insects are the only invertebrates that can fly.

26. C
From the passage, "some adult insects live underwater and are excellent swimmers."

27. D
From the passage, "Many insects communicate with sound."

28. A
Insects use their wings to attract a mate and drive off other males.

29. C
Insects are mostly solitary, but some are social like ants and bees.

30. A
Choice A is a re-wording of text from the passage.

31. B
This is taken directly from the passage.

32. C
Although trees are used as a building material, this is not their primary use. Trees are a primary energy source.

33. A
This is taken directly from the passage.

34. D
This question is designed to confuse by presenting different options for the 2 chemicals, oxygen and carbon dioxide. One is produced and one is reduced.

35. B
The inference is Botanists haven't surveyed all of the tropical areas so they don't know the number of species.

36. A
This is taken directly from the passage.

37. D
Tree ferns have survived from the Carboniferous period.

38. B
The different names depend on the vegetation and the local English dialect.

39. C
Wildfires are different because of their size and speed and also because of their ability to 'jump' gaps such as roads.

40. C
Wildfires are common in Australia due to the hot dry climate.

How to Take an Oral Exam

About oral exams

For many students, the experience of taking an oral exam is one that is very different to taking a written exam, although you may find that preparation for an oral exam is similar to a written exam.

An oral exam allows you to demonstrate to the assessor a variety of skills including:

- Speaking skills

- Presentation skills

- Communication skills

There are two typical types of oral exams, formal and informal. A formal oral exam will usually have a set of questions that have been prepared beforehand and these are often 'competitive' exams. An informal oral exam often has less structure and gives you a chance to elaborate on your answers.

Your assessor may construct a question based on an answer that you have just given to an earlier question and your assessor may be looking for you to demonstrate other skills in your answers, such as problem solving skills.

- Questions in oral exams are usually open-ended, which means that they require evaluative answers, not just six or seven words.

- Sometimes an oral exam will look for how much knowledge you may have around your subject.

Preparing for an Oral Exam

There are two main steps for preparing for an oral exam. They are revise and practice.

Revise

Like a written exam, you will not know what questions there are in an oral exam, so it is important that you revise fully beforehand.

Make a list of what you will need to revise and make sure that you spend more time revising your weaker topics. Try to make a study plan that covers all topics in the revision time you have available.

Rather than just revising individual topics, try to think about how these topics relate to each other, for example, X works because Y has certain components that X needs for it to work properly.

There are many approaches to revising for any exam, including:

Using index cards to write bullet points

- Writing key points on post-it's and sticking them around the house

- Recording notes and playing them back

- Using family and friends to help you revise

There is no right way of revising for everyone; you should consider what has worked for you in the past, with both oral and written exams.

- Never leave your revision until last minute.

- Think about possible questions for your subject.

- Take time to answer some practice questions.

- Get a friend to ask you some questions (this way you have no idea what they will ask you).

Practice

As well as revision, it is also important to practice for an oral exam. You can find it useful to practice in front of a mirror; this shows what habits you have when speaking to other people, such as playing with your hair, or fidgeting.

If you can, you should also take the opportunity to record yourself, as it is good for you to hear what you sound like.

• Practice speaking about your subject in front of other people.

• Practice speaking loud enough for everyone to hear.

• Practice speaking slower, you may find that you rush through an oral test because being nervous can make you talk faster.

• Practice speaking in full sentences.

If English is your second language then make sure that you speak English to as many people around you as possible. You should also take the opportunity to watch English TV, films and listen to the radio.

The Oral Exam

Before:

Always be there early, make sure you confirm the time, date and location of your exam beforehand.

• Switch your phone off.

• Be smart, some people choose to approach an oral exam like a job interview and just like an interview, first appearances are always important.

• It can help if you spend a few minutes before the exam relaxing. Try taking a deep breath in and as you breathe out, count one. Repeat this up to ten. This should help you to calm down.

• If you are using equipment such as a computer or pro-jector in your oral exam, check that everything works be-forehand.

During:

• Be confident and remember to smile.

• Try to maintain eye contact with your assessor.

• Always sit up properly.

You may find it helps if you have a slight pause and take a deep breath before you start speaking.

• Listen to everything that your assessor says.

• If you do not fully understand the question, ask your assessor to repeat it.

• Avoid rambling; tell your assessor if you do not know the answer.

• If you find your nerves have taken control of you, then ask your assessor if you may take a short pause for a drink of water.

• Always say thank you to the assessor at the end of the exam.

After your oral exam

You should always take time to sit down with a pen and paper straight after your oral exam. Jot down how well you thought you did and how you could improve in your next oral exam. This is important, as it will help you to improve your technique for future oral exams.

When you receive your mark and feedback, if you are not sure of why you have the mark that you do, ask your assessor or teacher for more detailed feedback.

How to Prepare for a Test

MOST STUDENTS HIDE THEIR HEADS AND PROCRASTINATE WHEN FACED WITH PREPARING FOR AN EXAMINATION, HOPING THAT SOMEHOW THEY WILL BE SPARED THE AGONY OF TAKING THAT TEST, ESPECIALLY IF IT IS A BIG ONE THAT THEIR FUTURES RELY ON. Avoiding the all-important test is what many students do best and unfortunately, they suffer the consequences because of their lack of preparation.

Test preparation requires strategy. It also requires a dedication to getting the job done. It is the perfect training ground for anyone planning a professional life. Besides having several reliable strategies, the wise student also has a clear goal in mind and knows how to accomplish it. These tried and true concepts have worked well and will make your test preparation easier.

The Study Approach.

Take responsibility for your own test preparation.

It is a common- but big - mistake to link your studying to someone else's. Study partners are great, but only if they are reliable. It is your job to be prepared for the test, even if a study partner fails you. Do not allow others to distract you from your goals.

Prioritize the time available to study.

When do you learn best, early in the day or in the dark of night? Does your mind absorb and retain information most efficiently in small blocks of time, or do you require long stretches to get the most done? It is important to figure out the best blocks of time available to you when you can be the most productive. Try to consolidate activities to allow for longer periods of study time.

Find a quiet place where you will not be disturbed.

Do not try to squeeze in quality study time in any old location. Find some place peaceful and with a minimum of distractions, such as the library, a park or even the laundry room. Good lighting is essential and you need to have comfortable seating and a desk surface large enough to hold your materials. It is probably not a great idea to study in your bedroom. You might be distracted by clothes on the floor, a book you have been planning to read, the telephone or something else. Besides, in the middle of studying, that bed will start to look very comfortable. Whatever you do, avoid using the bed as a place to study since you might fall asleep as a way of avoiding your work! That is the last thing that you should be doing during study time.

The exception is flashcards. By far the most productive study time is sitting down and studying and studying only. However, with flashcards you can carry them with you and make use of odd moments, like standing in line or waiting for the bus. This isn't as productive, but it really helps and is definately worth doing.

Determine what you need to study.

Gather together your books, your notes, your laptop and any other materials needed to focus on your study for this exam. Ensure you have everything you need so you don't waste time. Remember paper, pencils and erasers, sticky notes, bottled water and a snack. Keep your phone with you if you need it to find out essential information, but keep it turned off so others can't distract you.

Have a positive attitude.

It is essential that you approach your studies for the test with an attitude that says you will pass it. And pass it with flying colors! This is one of the most important keys to successful study strategy. Believing that you are capable actually helps you to become capable.

THE STRATEGY OF STUDYING

Make materials easy to review and access.

Consolidate materials to help keep your study area clutter free. If you have a laptop and a means of getting on line, you do not need a dictionary and thesaurus as well since those things are easily accessible via the internet. Go through written notes and consolidate those, as well. Have everything you need, but do not weigh yourself down with duplicates.

Review class notes.

Stay on top of class notes and assignments by reviewing them frequently. Re-writing notes can be a terrific study trick, as it helps lock in information. Pay special attention to any comments that have been made by the teacher. If a study guide has been made available as part of the class materials, use it! It will be a valuable tool to use for studying.

Estimate how much time you will need.

If you are concerned about the amount of time you have available it is a good idea to set up a schedule so that you do not get bogged down on one section and end without enough time left to study other things. Remember to schedule break time, and use that time for a little exercise or other stress reducing techniques.

Test yourself to determine your weaknesses.

Look online for additional assessment and evaluation tools available for a particular subject. Once you have determined areas of concern, you will be able to focus on studying the information they contain and just brush up on the other areas of the exam.

Mental Prep – How to Psych Yourself Up for a Test

Because tests contribute mightily to your final class grade or to whether you are accepted into a program, it is understandable that taking tests can create a great deal of anxiety for many students. Even students who know they have learned all the required material find their minds going blank as they stare at the words in the questions. One easy way to overcome that anxiety is to prepare mentally for the test. Mentally preparing for an exam is really not difficult. There are simple techniques that any student can learn to increase their chances of earning a great score on the day of the test.

Do not procrastinate.

Study the material for the test when it becomes available, and continue to review the material until the test day. By waiting until the last minute and trying to cram for the test the night before, you actually increase the amount of anxiety you feel. This leads to an increase in negative self-talk. Telling yourself "I can't learn this. I am going to fail" is a pretty sure indication that you are right. At best, your performance on the test will not be as strong if you have procrastinated instead of studying.

Positive self-talk.

Positive self-talk serves both to drown out negative self-talk and to increase your confidence in your abilities. Whenever you begin feeling overwhelmed or anxious about the test, remind yourself that you have studied enough, you know the material and that you will pass the test. Use only positive words. Both negative and positive self-talk are really just your fantasy, so why not choose to be a winner?

Do not compare yourself to anyone else.

Do not compare yourself to other students, or your performance to theirs. Instead, focus on your own strengths and weaknesses and prepare accordingly. Regardless of how others perform, your performance is the only one that matters to your grade. Comparing yourself to others increases your anxiety and your level of negative self-talk before the test.

Visualize.

Make a mental image of yourself taking the test. You know the answers and feel relaxed. Visualize doing well on the test and having no problems with the material. Visualizations can increase your confidence and decrease the anxiety you might otherwise feel before the test. Instead of thinking of this as a test, see it as an opportunity to demonstrate what you have learned!

Avoid negativity.

Worry is contagious and viral - once it gets started it builds on itself. Cut it off before it gets to be a problem. Even if you are relaxed and confident, being around anxious, worried classmates might cause you to start feeling anxious. Before the test, tune out the fears of classmates. Feeling anxious and worried before an exam is normal, and every student experiences those feelings at some point. But you cannot allow these feelings to interfere with your ability to perform well. Practicing mental preparation techniques and remembering that the test is not the only measure of your academic performance will ease your anxiety and ensure that you perform at your best.

How to Take a Test

EVERYONE KNOWS THAT TAKING AN EXAM IS STRESSFUL, BUT IT DOES NOT HAVE TO BE THAT BAD! There are a few simple things that you can do to increase your score on any type of test. Take a look at these tips and consider how you can incorporate them into your study time.

Reading the Instructions

This is the most basic point, but one that, surprisingly, many students ignore and it can cost them big time! Since reading the instructions is one of the most common, and 100% preventable mistakes, we have a whole section just on reading instructions.

Pay close attention to the sample questions. Almost all standardized tests offer sample questions, paired with their correct solutions. Go through these to make sure that you understand what they mean and how they arrived at the correct answer. Do not be afraid to ask the test supervisor for help with a sample that confuses you, or instructions that you are unsure of.

Tips for Reading the Question

We could write pages and pages of tips just on reading the test questions. Here are the ones that will help you the most.

- **Think first.** Before you look at the answer, read and think about the question. It is best to try to come up with the correct answer before you look at the options given. This way, when the test-writer tries to trick you with a close answer, you will not fall for it.

- **Make it true or false.** If a question confuses you, then look at each answer option and think of it as a "true" "false" question. Select the one that seems most likely to be "true."

- **Mark the Question.** For some reason, a lot of test-takers are afraid to mark up their test booklet. Unless you are specifically told not to mark in the booklet, you should feel free to use it to your advantage. More on this below.

- **Circle Key Words.** As you are reading the question, underline or circle key words. This helps you to focus on the most critical information needed to solve the problem. For example, if the question said, "Which of these is not a synonym for huge?" You might circle "not," "synonym" and "huge." That clears away the clutter and lets you focus on what is important. More on this below.

- **Always underline these words:** all, none, always, never, most, best, true, false and except.

- **Cross out irrelevant choices.** If you find yourself confused by lengthy questions, cross out anything that you think is irrelevant, obviously wrong, or information that you think is offered to distract you.

- **Do not try to read between the lines.** Usually, questions are written to be straightforward, with no deep, underlying meaning. The simple answer really is often the correct answer. Do not over-analyze!

How to Take a Test - The Basics

Some tests are designed to assess your ability to quickly grab the necessary information; this type of exam makes speed a priority. Others are more concerned with your depth of knowledge, and how accurate it is. When you receive a test, look it over to determine whether the test is for speed or accuracy. If the test is for speed, like many standardized tests, your strategy is clear; answer as many questions as quickly as possible.

Watch out, though! There are a few tests that are designed to determine how fully and accurately you can answer the questions. Guessing on this type of test is a big mistake, because the teacher expects any student with an average grade to be able to complete the test in the time given. Racing through the test and making guesses that prove to be incorrect will cost you big time!

Make time your friend.

Budget your time from the moment your pencil hits the page until you are finished with the exam, and stick to it! Virtually all standardized tests have a time limit for each section. The amount of time you are permitted for each portion of the test will almost certainly be included in the instructions or printed at the top of the page. If for some reason it is not immediately visible, rather than wasting your time hunting for it you can use the points or percentage of the score as a proxy to make an educated guess regarding the time limit.

Use the allotted time for each section and then move onto the next section whether you have completed the first section or not. Stick with the instructions and you will be able to answer most the questions in each section.

With speed tests you may not be able to complete the entire test. Rest assured that you are not really expected to! The goal of this type of examination is to determine how quickly you can reach into your brain and access a particular piece of information, which is one way of determining how well you know it. If you know a test you are taking is a speed test, you will know the strategies to use for the best results.

Easy does it.

One smart way to tackle a test is to locate the easy questions and answer those first. This is a time-tested strategy that never fails, because it saves you a lot of unnecessary fretting. First, read the question and decide if you can answer it in less than a minute. If so, complete the question and go to the next one. If not, skip it for now and continue to the next question. By the time you have completed the first pass through this section of the exam, you will have answered a good number of questions. Not only does it boost your confidence, relieve anxiety and kick your memory up a notch, you will know exactly how many questions remain and can allot the rest of your time accordingly. Think of doing the easy questions first as a warm-up!

If you run out of time before you manage to tackle all the difficult questions, do not let it throw you. All that means is you have used your time in the most efficient way possible by answering as many questions correctly as you could. Missing a few points by not answering a question whose answer you do not know just means you spent that time answering one whose answer you did.

A word to the wise: Skipping questions for which you are drawing a complete blank is one thing, but we are not suggesting you skip every question you come across that you are not 100 % certain of. A good rule of thumb is to try to answer at least eight of every 10 questions the first time through.

Do not watch your watch.

At best, taking an important exam is an uncomfortable situation. If you are like most people, you might be tempted to subconsciously distract yourself from the task at hand. One of the most common ways to do so is by becoming obsessed with your watch or the wall clock. Do not watch your watch! Take it off and place it on the top corner of your desk, far enough away that you will not be tempted to look at it every two minutes. Better still, turn the watch face away from you. That way, every time you try to sneak a peek, you will be reminded to refocus your attention to the task at hand. Give yourself permission to check your watch or the wall clock after you complete each section. If you know yourself to be a bit of a slow-poke in other aspects of life, you can check your watch a bit more often. Even so, focus on answering the questions, not on how many minutes have elapsed since you last looked at it.

Divide and conquer.

What should you do when you come across a question that is so complicated you may not even be certain what is being asked? As we have suggested, the first time through the section you are best off skipping the question. But at some point, you will need to return to it and get it under control. The best way to handle questions that leave you feeling so anxious you can hardly think is by breaking them into manageable pieces. Solving smaller bits is always easier. For complicated questions, divide them into bite-sized pieces and solve these smaller sets separately. Once you understand what the reduced sections are really saying, it will be much easier to put them together and get a handle on the bigger question.

Reason your way through the toughest questions.

If you find that a question is so dense you can't figure out how to break it into smaller pieces, there are a few strategies that might help. First, read the question again and look for hints. Can you re-word the question in one or more different ways? This may give you clues. Look for words that can function as either verbs or nouns, and try to figure out from the sentence structure which it is here. Remember that many nouns in English have several different meanings. While some of those meanings might be related, sometimes they are completely distinct. If reading the sentence one way does not make sense, consider a different definition or meaning for a key word.

The truth is, it is not always necessary to understand a question to arrive at a correct answer! A trick that successful students understand is using Strategy 5, Elimination. Frequently, at least one answer is clearly wrong and can be crossed off the list of possible correct answers. Next, look at the remaining answers and eliminate any that are only partially true. You may still have to flat-out guess from time to time, but using the process of elimination will help you make your way to the correct answer more often than not - even when you don't know what the question means!

Do not leave early.

Use all the time allotted to you, even if you can't wait to get out of the testing room. Instead, once you have finished, spend the remaining time reviewing your answers. Go back to those questions that were most difficult for you and review your response. Another good way to use this time is to return to multiple-choice questions in which you filled in a bubble. Do a spot check, reviewing every fifth or sixth question to make sure your answer coincides with the bubble you filled in. This is a great way to catch yourself if you made a mistake, skipped a bubble and therefore put all your answers in the wrong bubbles!

Become a super sleuth and look for careless errors. Look for questions that have double negatives or other odd phrasing; they might be an attempt to throw you off. Careless errors on your part might be the result of skimming a question and missing a key word. Words such as "always," "never," "sometimes", "rarely" and the like can give a strong indication of the answer the question is really seeking. Don't throw away points by being careless!

Just as you budgeted time at the beginning of the test to allow for easy and more difficult questions, be sure to budget sufficient time to review your answers. On essay questions and math questions where you are required to show your work, check your writing to make sure it is legible.

Here is another terrific tip. It is likely that no matter how hard you try, you will have a handful of questions you just are not sure of. Keep them in mind as you read through the rest of the test. If you can't answer a question, looking back over the test to find a different question that addresses the same topic might give you clues.

We know that taking the test has been stressful and you can hardly wait to escape. Just keep in mind that leaving before you double-check as much as possible can be a quick trip to disaster. Taking a few extra minutes can make the difference between getting a bad grade and a great one. Besides, there will be lots of time to relax and celebrate after the test is turned in.

In the Test Room – What you MUST do!

If you are like the rest of the world, there is almost nothing you would rather avoid than taking a test. Unfortunately, that is not an option if you want to pass. Rather than suffer, consider a few attitude adjustments that might turn the experience from a horrible one to...well, an interesting one! Take a look at these tips. Simply changing how you perceive the experience can change the experience itself.

Get in the mood.

After weeks of studying, the big day has finally arrived. The worst thing you can do to yourself is arrive at the test site feeling frustrated, worried, and anxious. Keep a check on your emotional state. If your emotions are shaky before a test it can determine how well you do on the test. It is extremely important that you pump yourself up, believe in yourself, and use that confidence to get in the mood!

Don't fight reality.

Oftentimes, students resent tests, and with good reason. After all, many people do not test well, and they know the grade they end with does not accurately reflect their true knowledge. It is easy to feel resentful because tests classify students and create categories that just don't seem fair. Face it: Students who are great at rote memorization and not that good at actually analyzing material often score higher than those who might be more creative thinkers and balk at simply memorizing cold, hard facts. It may not be fair, but there it is anyway. Conformity is an asset on tests, and creativity is often a liability. There is no point in wasting time or energy being upset about this reality. Your first step is to accept the reality and get used to it. You will get higher marks when you realize tests do count and that you must give them your best effort. Think about your future and the career that is easier to achieve if you have consistently earned high grades. Avoid negative energy and focus on anything that lifts your enthusiasm and increases your motivation.

Get there early enough to relax.

If you are wound up, tense, scared, anxious, or feeling rushed, it will cost you. Get to the exam room early and relax before you go in. This way, when the exam starts, you are comfortable and ready to apply yourself. Of course, you do not want to arrive so early that you are the only one there. That will not help you relax; it will only give you too much time to sit there, worry and get wound up all over again.

If you can, visit the room where you will be taking your exam a few days ahead of time. Having a visual image of the room can be surprisingly calming, because it takes away one of the big 'unknowns'. Not only that, but once you have visited, you know how to get there and will not be worried about getting lost. Furthermore, driving to the test site once lets you know how much time you need to allow for the trip. That means three potential stressors have been eliminated all at once.

Get it down on paper.

One of the advantages of arriving early is that it allows you time to recreate notes. If you spend a lot of time worrying about whether you will be able to remember information like names, dates, places, and mathematical formulas, there is a solution for that. Unless the exam you are taking allows you to use your books and notes, (and very few do) you will have to rely on memory. Arriving early gives to time to tap into your memory and jot down key pieces of information you know will be asked. Just make certain you are allowed to make notes once you are in the testing site; not all locations will permit it. Once you get your test, on a small piece of paper write down everything you are afraid you will forget. It will take a minute or two but by dumping your worries onto the page you have effectively eliminated a certain amount of anxiety and driven off the panic you feel.

Get comfortable in your chair.

Here is a clever technique that releases physical stress and helps you get comfortable, even relaxed in your body. You will tense and hold each of your muscles for just a few seconds. The trick is, you must tense them hard for the technique to work. You might want to practice this technique a few times at home; you do not want an unfamiliar technique to add to your stress just before a test, after all! Once you are at the test site, this exercise can always be done in the rest room or another quiet location.

Start with the muscles in your face then work down your body. Tense, squeeze and hold the muscles for a moment or two. Notice the feel of every muscle as you go down your body. Scowl to tense your forehead, pull in your chin to tense your neck. Squeeze your shoulders down to tense your back. Pull in your stomach all the way back to your ribs, make your lower back tight then stretch your fingers. Tense your leg muscles and calves then stretch your feet and your toes. You should be as stiff as a board throughout your entire body.

Now relax your muscles in reverse starting with your toes. Notice how all the muscles feel as you relax them one by one. Once you have released a muscle or set of muscles, allow them to remain relaxed as you proceed up your body. Focus on how you are feeling as all the tension leaves. Start breathing deeply when you get to your chest muscles. By the time you have found your chair, you will be so relaxed it will feel like bliss!

Fight distraction.

A lucky few are able to focus deeply when taking an important examination, but most people are easily distracted, probably because they would rather be anyplace else! There are a number of things you can do to protect yourself from distraction.

Stay away from windows. If you select a seat near a window you may end gazing out at the landscape instead of paying attention to the work at hand. Furthermore, any sign of human activity, from a single individual walking by to a couple having an argument or exchanging a kiss will draw your attention away from your important work. What goes on outside should not be allowed to distract you.

Choose a seat away from the aisle so you do not become distracted by people who leave early. People who leave the exam room early are often the ones who fail. Do not compare your time to theirs.

Of course, you love your friends; that's why they are your friends! In the test room, however, they should become complete strangers inside your mind. Forget they are there. The first step is to physically distance yourself from friends or classmates. That way, you will not be tempted to glance at them to see how they are doing, and there will be no chance of eye contact that could either distract you or even lead to an accusation of cheating. Furthermore, if they are feeling stressed because they did not spend the focused time studying that you did, their anxiety is less likely to permeate your hard-earned calm.

Of course, you will want to choose a seat where there is sufficient light. Nothing is worse than trying to take an important examination under flickering lights or dim bulbs.

Ask the instructor or exam proctor to close the door if there is a lot of noise outside. If the instructor or proctor is unable to do so, block out the noise as best you can. Do not let anything disturb you.

Make sure you have enough pencils, pens and whatever else you will need. Many entrance exams do not permit you to bring personal items such as candy bars into the testing room. If this is the case with the exam you are sitting for, be sure to eat a nutritionally balanced breakfast. Eat protein, complex carbohydrates and a little fat to keep you feeling full and to supercharge your energy. Nothing is worse than a sudden drop in blood sugar during an exam.

Do not allow yourself to become distracted by being too cold or hot. Regardless of the weather outside, carry a sweater, scarf or jacket if the air conditioning at the test site is set too high, or the heat set too low. By the same token, dress in layers so that you are prepared for a range of temperatures.

Bring a watch so that you can keep track of time management. The danger here is many students become obsessed with how many minutes have passed since the last question. Instead of wearing the watch, remove it and place it in the far upper corner of the desk with the face turned away. That way, you cannot become distracted by repeatedly glancing at the time, but it is available if you need to know it.

Drinking a gallon of coffee or gulping a few energy drinks might seem like a great idea, but it is, in fact, a very bad one. Caffeine, pep pills or other artificial sources of energy are more likely to leave you feeling rushed and ragged. Your brain might be clicking along, all right, but chances are good it is not clicking along on the right track! Furthermore, drinking lots of coffee or energy drinks will mean frequent trips to the rest room. This will cut into the time you should be spending answering questions and is a distraction in itself, since each time you need to leave the room you lose focus. Pep pills will only make it harder for you to think straight when solving complicated problems on the exam.

At the same time, if anxiety is your problem try to find ways around using tranquilizers during test-taking time. Even medically prescribed anti-anxiety medication can make you less alert and even decrease your motivation. Being motivated is what you need to get you through an exam. If your anxiety is so bad that it threatens to interfere with your ability to take an exam, speak to your doctor and ask for documentation. Many testing sites will allow non-distracting test rooms, extended testing time and other accommodations as long as a doctor's note that explains the situation is made available.

Keep Breathing.

It might not make a lot of sense, but when people become anxious, tense, or scared, their breathing becomes shallow and, in some cases, they stop breathing all together! Pay attention to your emotions, and when you are feeling worried, focus on your breathing. Take a moment to remind yourself to breathe deeply and regularly. Drawing in steady, deep breaths energizes the body. When you continue to breathe deeply you will notice you exhale all the tension.

It is a smart idea to rehearse breathing at home. With continued practice of this relaxation technique, you will begin to know the muscles that tense up under pressure. Call these your "signal muscles." These are the ones that will speak to you first, begging you to relax. Take the time to listen to those muscles and do as they ask. With just a little breathing practice, you will get into the habit of checking yourself regularly and when you realize you are tense, relaxation will become second nature.

Avoid Anxiety Before a Test

Manage your time effectively.

This is a key to your success! You need blocks of uninterrupted time to study all the pertinent material. Creating and maintaining a schedule will help keep you on track, and will remind family members and friends that you are not available. Under no circumstances should you change your blocks of study time to accommodate someone else, or cancel a study session to do something more fun. Do not interfere with your study time for any reason!

Relax.

Use whatever works best for you to relieve stress. Some folks like a good, calming stretch with yoga, others find expressing themselves through journaling to be useful. Some hit the floor for a series of crunches or planks, and still others take a slow stroll around the garden. Integrate a little relaxation time into your schedule, and treat that time, too, as sacred.

Eat healthy.

Instead of reaching for the chips and chocolate, fresh fruits and vegetables are not only yummy but offer nutritional benefits that help to relieve stress. Some foods accelerate stress instead of reducing it and should be avoided. Foods that add to higher anxiety include artificial sweeteners, candy and other sugary foods, carbonated sodas, chips, chocolate, eggs, fried foods, junk foods, processed foods, red meat, and other foods containing preservatives or heavy spices. Instead, eat a bowl of berries and some yogurt!

Get plenty of ZZZZZZZs.

Do not cram or try to do an all-nighter. If you created a study schedule at the beginning, and if you have stuck with that schedule, have confidence! Staying up too late trying to cram in last-minute bits of information is going to leave you exhausted the next day. Besides, whatever new information you cram in will only displace all the important ideas you've spent weeks learning. Remember: You need to be alert and fully functional the day of the exam

Have confidence in yourself!

Everyone experiences some anxiety when taking a test, but exhibiting a positive attitude banishes anxiety and fills you with the knowledge you really do know what you need to know. This is your opportunity to show how well prepared you are. Go for it!

Do not chitchat with friends.

Let your friends know ahead of time that it is not anything personal, but you are going to ignore them in the test room! You need to find a seat away from doors and windows, one that has good lighting, and get comfortable. If other students are worried their anxiety could be detrimental to you; of course, you do not have to tell your friends that. If you are afraid they will be offended, tell them you are protecting them from your anxiety!

Common Test-Taking Mistakes

Taking a test is not much fun at best. When you take a test and make a stupid mistake that negatively affects your grade, it is natural to be very upset, especially when it is something that could have been easily avoided. So what are some of the common mistakes that are made on tests?

Do not fail to put your name on the test.

How could you possibly forget to put your name on a test? You would be amazed at how often that happens. Very often, tests without names are thrown out immediately, resulting in a failing grade.

Marking the wrong multiple-choice answer.

It is important to work at a steady pace, but that does not mean bolting through the questions. Be sure the answer you are marking is the one you mean to. If the bubble you need to fill in or the answer you need to circle is 'C', do not allow yourself to get distracted and select 'B' instead.

Answering a question twice.

Some multiple-choice test questions have two very similar answers. If you are in too much of a hurry, you might select them both. Remember that only one answer is correct, so if you choose more than one, you have automatically failed that question.

Mishandling a difficult question.

We recommend skipping difficult questions and returning to them later, but beware! First, be certain that you do return to the question. Circling the entire passage or placing a large question mark beside it will help you spot it when you are reviewing your test. Secondly, if you are not careful to skip the question, you can mess yourself up badly. Imagine that a question is too difficult and you decide to save it for later. You read the next question, which you know the answer to, and you fill in that answer. You continue to the end of the test then return to the difficult question only to discover you didn't actually skip it! Instead, you inserted the answer to the following question in the spot reserved for the harder one, thus throwing off the remainder of your test!

Incorrectly Transferring an answer from scratch paper.

This can happen easily if you are trying to hurry! Double check any answer you have figured out on scratch paper, and make sure what you have written on the test itself is an exact match!

Don't ignore the clock, and don't marry it, either.

In a timed examination many students lose track of the time and end up without sufficient time to complete the test. Remember to pace yourself! At the same time, though, do not allow yourself to become obsessed with how much time has elapsed, either.

Thinking too much.

Oftentimes, your first thought is your best thought. If you worry yourself into insecurity, your self-doubts can trick you into choosing an incorrect answer when your first impulse was the right one!

Be prepared.

Running out of ink and not having an extra pen or pencil is not an excuse for failing an exam! Have everything you need, and have extras. Bring tissue, an extra eraser, several sharpened pencils, batteries for electronic devices, and anything else you might need.

Not following directions.

Directions are carefully worded. If you skim directions, it is very easy to miss key words or misinterpret what is being said. Nothing is worse than failing an examination simply because you could not be bothered with reading the instructions!

Conclusion

CONGRATULATIONS! You have made it this far because you have applied yourself diligently to practicing for the exam and no doubt improved your potential score considerably! Passing your up-coming exam is a huge step in a journey that might be challenging at times but will be many times more rewarding and fulfilling. That is why being prepared is so important.

Good Luck!

Endnotes

READING COMPREHENSION PASSAGES WHERE NOTED BELOW ARE USED IN MODIFIED FORM UNDER THE CREATIVE COMMONS ATTRIBUTION-SHAREALIKE 3.0 LICENSE. For details visit,

http://en.wikipedia.org/wiki/Wikipedia:Text_of_Creative_Commons_Attribution-ShareAlike_3.0_Unported_License

[1] What is Free Range Chicken In *Answers.com*. Retrieved Feb 14, 2009, from http://wiki.answers.com/Q/What_is_free-range_chicken.

[2] Grizzly Bear. In *Wikipedia*. Retrieved Feb 14, 2009, from http://en.wikipedia.org/wiki/Grizzly_Bear.

[3] Grizzly Polar Bear Hybrid. In *Wikipedia*. Retrieved Feb 14, 2009, from http://en.wikipedia.org/wiki/Grizzly%E2%80%93polar_bear_hybrid.

[4] Peafowl. In *Wikipedia*. Retrieved Feb 14, 2009, from en.wikipedia.org/wiki/Peafowl.

[5] Smallpox. In *Wikipedia*. Retrieved Feb 14, 2009, from http://en.wikipedia.org/wiki/Smallpox.

[6] Lightning. In *Wikipedia*. Retrieved Feb 14, 2009, from http://en.wikipedia.org/wiki/Lightning.

[7] Venus. In *Wikipedia*. Retrieved Feb 14, 2009, from http://en.wikipedia.org/wiki/Venus.

[8] Weather. In *Wikipedia*. Retrieved Feb 14, 2009, from http://en.wikipedia.org/wiki/Weather.

[10] Ebola. In *Wikipedia*. Retrieved Feb 14, 2009, from http://en.wikipedia.org/wiki/Ebola.

[11] Fruit Bat. In *Wikipedia*. Retrieved Feb 14, 2009, from http://en.wikipedia.org/wiki/Fruit_Bat.

[12] Gardens. In *Wikipedia*. Retrieved Feb 14, 2009, from http://en.wikipedia.org/wiki/Gardens.

[13] Insects. In *Wikipedia*. Retrieved Feb 14, 2009, from http://en.wikipedia.org/wiki/Insects.

[14] Insects. In *Wikipedia*. Retrieved Feb 14, 2009, from http://en.wikipedia.org/wiki/Insects.

[15] Trees. In *Wikipedia*. Retrieved Feb 14, 2009, from http://en.wikipedia.org/wiki/Trees.

Visit Us Online!

Taking a test? We can help!

**Complete study guides, practice test
test questions, study tips and more:**

www.test-preparation.ca

CPSIA information can be obtained
at www.ICGtesting.com
Printed in the USA
FSHW04n0944260318
46123FS